W9-BNW-200

SISTER JANET

SISTER JANET

*Nurse and Heroine of the
Anglo-Zulu War*

by

Brian Best
&
Katie Stossel

Pen & Sword
MILITARY

First published in Great Britain in 2006 by
Pen & Sword Military
an imprint of
Pen & Sword Books Ltd
47 Church Street
Barnsley
South Yorkshire
S70 2AS

Copyright © Debinair Publishing Ltd., 2006

ISBN 1 84415 425 4
978 1 84415 425 8

The right of Adrian Greaves to be identified as Editor of this Work has
been asserted by him in accordance with the Copyright,
Designs and Patents Act 1988.

A CIP catalogue record for this book is
available from the British Library

All rights reserved. No part of this book may be reproduced or
transmitted in any form or by any means, electronic or mechanical
including photocopying, recording or by any information storage and
retrieval system, without permission from the Publisher in writing.

Typeset in Sabon by
Phoenix Typesetting, Auldgirth, Dumfriesshire

Printed and bound in England by
Biddles Ltd., King's Lynn

Pen & Sword Books Ltd incorporates the Imprints of Pen & Sword
Aviation, Pen & Sword Maritime, Pen & Sword Military, Wharncliffe
Local History, Pen & Sword Select, Pen & Sword Military Classics and
Leo Cooper.

For a complete list of Pen & Sword titles please contact
PEN & SWORD BOOKS LIMITED
47 Church Street, Barnsley, South Yorkshire, S70 2AS, England
E-mail: enquiries@pen-and-sword.co.uk
Website: www.pen-and-sword.co.uk

Contents

Acknowledgements

The publication of this book was first considered in 1880 by a young English nurse, Sister Janet Wells, on her arrival home from two major wars, the Russo-Turkish Balkan War of 1877–8 and the South African Anglo Zulu War of 1879. She was just twenty years old. Her remarkable deeds and bravery were duly acknowledged by Queen Victoria with the award of the Royal Red Cross decoration and by the Russian government with the Imperial Red Cross of Russia. Due to the exigencies of the time and her ongoing nursing duties, followed by her marriage to a successful newspaper editor, her remarkable story remained unpublished and largely unknown outside her family.

Then, in 2003, her direct great-granddaughter, Mrs Susie Cooper, re-discovered Sister Janet's scrapbooks and her personal effects relating to the Anglo Zulu War. The role of Susie Cooper in bringing this remarkable story to the attention of *The Anglo Zulu War Historical Society* is acknowledged with sincere thanks. Without Susie's generosity and willing assistance to make this material available, Sister Janet's story could not be told.

As editor, I also acknowledge the two years of detailed research and work to assemble the story by the book's two enthusiastic authors. Both visited relevant locations in the UK and Zululand. Brian Best, chairman of the Victoria Cross Society, researched the background to events that brought Sister Janet to nursing and her subsequent career. Katie Stossel SRN, a former operating theatre sister, prepared the nursing and personal side of Janet's life, ably

vii

assisted by her Consultant Surgeon husband Clifford who helped with the research of the medical records, the preparation and photography of the South Africa field medical kit and the restoration of the 1870s photographs of Tottenham Hospital. My task as editor, was made easy by their diligent research. I also thank Geoff Fawcett and Jenny Martin for their advice in compiling the book and Anna Maplesden and her husband, Mark, for enthusiastically searching out and accompanying me to relevant locations in Zululand.

Other thanks go to David and Nicky Rattray for the use of the Mangeni photograph and wonderful hospitality at their Fugitives' Drift Lodge during our lengthy research, and especially to Robert Waite, assistant curator of Haringey Libraries, Archives and Museums, for his kind permission to use their excellent Victorian hospital photographs.

Dr Adrian Greaves, Editor

Foreword

The Anglo Zulu War of 1879 caused many British soldiers and Zulu warriors terrible wounds, and disease was rife. Hospital care was in its infancy, especially in the British Army, and so it is remarkable that in the midst of this terrible war a nineteen year-old English nurse, Sister Janet Wells, was sent from London to take charge of the isolated and overcrowded British Army hospital at Utrecht in South Africa. Already a decorated veteran of the 1878 Balkan War, she was highly experienced in treating war wounds. In her first two months at Utrecht she treated over 3,200 patients, both British soldiers and Zulus, many from the battles of Hlobane, Khambula and Ulundi.

She performed numerous operations, tended the sick and wounded, and brought an air of discipline, tempered by her charm and femininity, into a chaotic and desperate situation. Towards the end of the war she was sent to Rorke's Drift where she administered to the remaining garrison. She walked the battlefields of Rorke's Drift and Isandlwana where she collected flowers for her scrapbooks – already containing many sketches and photographs, which survive to this day.

After the war she returned to her home and family in London, just in time for her twentieth birthday. Recognition by Queen Victoria followed, who decorated her with the Royal Red Cross, which was then the nursing equivalent of the Victoria Cross. The previous recipient was Florence Nightingale.

Hers is an astonishing story, of bravery and determination,

which I commend to everyone who loves an adventure; it will especially fascinate students of the Anglo Zulu War – to whom this factual account will come, I am sure, as something of a surprise.

David Rattray
Fugitives' Drift Lodge
Zululand
South Africa

January 2006

By Queen Victoria's command

The profession of nursing, as we know it today, is relatively new. During the early 1870s the concept of young women of good background becoming nurses became more socially acceptable and so training hospitals and the Red Cross began to attract a growing number of dedicated single women to nursing. For the first time, women felt they could gain fulfilment by doing something that was both feminine and worthwhile. However, the strict training, based on Florence Nightingale's system of cleanliness and scrupulous attention to hygiene, discouraged those who had a woolly or sentimental concept of what nursing was about. Nurses' conditions were austere, working long hours and their training was rigorous and impartial.

After only a short period of training, one of these pioneering nurses, Janet Wells, aged only eighteen, was to undergo a remarkably tough baptism of fire from which she would emerge as one of the nursing heroines of the late Victorian era. Like other girls of her class, Janet Wells kept a scrapbook of newspaper clippings, photographs, sketches and pressed flowers, which chronicled her life on the battlefields like an illustrated diary. What emerges from the pages of her records and other contemporary material is the life of a young woman whose bravery, stamina and dedication to nursing were readily recognized by her peers and who, at the end of her all-too-short life, was hailed as an early nursing heroine alongside Florence Nightingale.

During her nursing career, in which she saw action in two major wars while still a teenager, she would undertake major surgery, care for thousands of wounded, fall in love, and yet retain her gaiety, charm and her high personal level of professionalism. She would mix with soldiers, generals and royalty with equal ease. She became known as an 'angel of mercy' by many whose lives she saved. Hers is a story as unusual as it is dramatic.

Janet Wells was born in 1859 at Shepherd's Bush, London, to Benjamin Wells, a noted musician of his time, and his wife Elizabeth. She was the second child of five daughters and three sons. During her childhood the family moved to Islington. In November 1876, aged seventeen years, she entered the emerging profession of nursing by joining the Evangelical Protestant Deaconesses' Institution and Training Hospital as a trainee nurse. On qualifying, she was immediately sent to the Balkans to assist the Russian army medical teams in the 1877–8 Russo-Turkish War. In the depths of a bitterly cold Russian winter she was thrust into an appallingly cruel war and required to treat many thousands of seriously wounded soldiers – frequently on her own and with scant medical backup or resources.

In early 1879 she returned to England but was immediately requested to go to South Africa. Alone, she was sent more than 200 miles across wild and unpopulated bush to take control of the most distant British Army medical post at Utrecht in Zululand, where she cared for sick and injured soldiers after the savage Anglo Zulu War. Following the peace declaration, she visited many of the famous battlefields, including Rorke's Drift and Isandlwana, where she administered medical care to the remaining British garrison. She also met and treated King Cetshwayo, then a prisoner of the British at Cape Town. On 28 October 1879 she departed from Cape Town for the return journey to England; her intention was to resume her nursing career. She was not yet twenty years old.

In 1880 she met Mr George King, an up and coming young London journalist who was soon to become the distinguished editor of the *Globe* magazine and founder of *Tatler*. They married in May 1882 and subsequently had two daughters, Elsie and Daisy.

Janet was widely recognized for her dedication to nursing; she received the Russian Imperial Order of the Red Cross for assisting the Russian army in the Balkans, the South Africa Campaign medal for her participation in the Anglo Zulu War and, in 1883, by Queen Victoria's command, she and Florence Nightingale were the very first recipients awarded the Royal Red Cross decoration for 'the special devotion and competency which you have displayed in your nursing duties with Her Majesty's Troops'. At the time, the Royal Red Cross was regarded as the nursing equivalent of the military and naval Victoria Cross. (see Appendix A)

In 1901, Queen Victoria died and Janet King RRC was invited to the state funeral. Janet died of cancer on 6 June 1911 at the age of fifty-three. Hers is an astonishing story, of bravery and determination, which I commend to everyone who loves an adventure; it will especially fascinate students of the Anglo Zulu War – to whom this factual account will come, I am sure, as something of a surprise.

The early life of this brave young nurse is inextricably bound up with a number of vicious wars that raged across Europe as well as with the protracted development and establishment of the Red Cross.

For those readers keen to gain a comprehensive overview of the situation, then Part I leads the way. Those more interested in the life and experiences of Janet Wells can turn to Part II to assuage their interest – before, no doubt, returning to Part I.

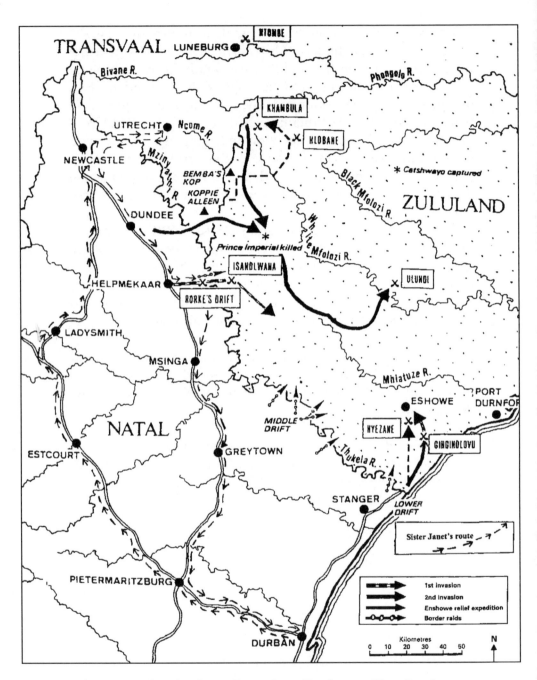

The route taken by Sister Janet from Durban to Utrecht, then on
to Rorke's Drift before returning to Durban. The routes shown
are all rough cart tracks: there were no roads in 1879.

PART I

Leading the Way

CHAPTER ONE

Enter Florence Nightingale

and the start of care for the casualties of war . . .

For all its destructiveness, war has paradoxically been responsible for great scientific and social advances. Communications and the media were revolutionized by the need to report conflicts swiftly, while many chemicals and materials that we use every day were developed because of war. The field of medical care was an area that cried out for change and it was due to war in the far-off Crimean peninsula in 1854 that brought this about. Not that the medical establishment sought change. Quite the reverse, it fought long and hard to maintain the status quo but was unable to resist the determination of a strong-willed woman to change forever the method of care for sick and wounded soldiers. This outstanding woman was, of course, Florence Nightingale.

In the summer of 1854 Russia and Turkey went to war on the strength of a petty squabble that had broken out concerning the guardianship of Christian holy places in the Holy Land, then part of the Ottoman Empire. Using this as a pretext to invade the Turkish provinces of Moldavia, Wallachia and Bulgaria that bordered the western shores of the Black Sea, Russia declared war. The destruction by the Russians of the Turkish fleet at anchor in the port of Sinope, which cost the Turks 4,000 lives, led to public outrage in Britain. The spectre of Russia gaining control of the Bosporus and having access to the Mediterranean began to look distinctly possible and it was a situation that neither Britain nor France could allow. The two old adversaries agreed on armed

3

intervention to support the Turks and during April and May 1854 they dispatched a large combined force of British and French troops to Varna in Bulgaria.

By the time they arrived, the Turks had managed to repulse the Russian invasion and the war had petered out. Thwarted, the allies sat in their cholera-ravaged camps around Varna un-decided as to what to do next. To have gone to the expense and trouble of sending their magnificently attired soldiers to fight the hated Russians and then to slink back home without doing battle was too shameful, so a fresh objective had to be found.

In November a joint British-French expeditionary force of 58,000 men was sent across 400 miles of the Black Sea to land on the west coast of the Crimean peninsula. From their beachhead, the allies would then attack and destroy the main Russian naval port of Sebastopol. The Russians showed a lack of enterprise by not attacking the vulnerable and ponderous flotilla that deposited its cargo of seasick soldiers on the open beach at the ominously named Calamita Bay, just thirty miles north of Sebastopol. In fact, seasickness was the least of the allies' worries for the soldiers carried the cholera virus with them from Varna, where the disease had stricken whole camps.

The allies, and the British in particular, were badly prepared for what was to come. Because of lack of space in the ships, they had left their medical supplies behind at Varna along with all their hospital marquees, ambulance wagons, pack animals, bedding, stretchers and kitchen equipment. A lack of transport when they landed meant that they had to march without tents. Before a shot was fired, over 2,000 men were sent off to the main hospital at Scutari on a ship that carried precious supplies but which had been unable to land any due to the administrative chaos.

Still unopposed and lacking any accurate maps of the region, the huge colourful cavalcade marched south towards their objec-tive. For those who were free from sickness, the journey into the Crimea was pleasant as the allies marched through the gently rolling autumn countryside, interrupted only by easily fordable streams that traversed the valleys. As they breasted the rise that led down to the River Alma, the allies saw their enemy for the first time. Arrayed on the heights on the far bank were the grey ranks of the Russian army. With little or no control and even less direction from the British commander, Lord Raglan, the British advanced under heavy fire and, despite serious losses, managed to cross the river. The Light Division then led the advance up the shell-swept slope and captured the earthwork housing the main Russian artillery. A determined Russian counter-attack forced the British back down the slope where they met the Brigade of Guards – who steadily pressed on through the withering hail of shot. With great bravery and determination, the Brigade captured the well-defended 'Great Redoubt' and shortly afterwards, the Russians quit the battlefield.

One of the soldiers who showed particular bravery that day was a twenty-two year-old officer in the Scots Fusilier Guards who unflinchingly carried the Queen's Colour and inspired all those around him. He was Lieutenant Robert James Loyd-Lindsay, who was later to play a significant role in the establishment of the British Red Cross. For his role at the Battle of the Alma, and later at Inkerman, Lindsay was awarded the Victoria Cross.

The allied victory on the Alma was not followed up with any pursuit even though the Russian army was clearly in disarray. To do so would have brought about the capture of Sebastopol and the war would have been over. Instead, the British, who had borne the brunt of the fighting, spent a forlorn night trying to cope with the large numbers of wounded who covered the slopes down to the river. With little or no medical supplies or equipment in the field, the wounded had to be carried on rough wooden carts to the mouth of the river from where they were rowed to the British fleet anchored offshore.

In his report to the Hospital Commissioners, Staff Surgeon T. Alexander of the Light Division described the impossible conditions that existed on the battlefield. There were no ambulances and, incredibly, no lanterns, so nearly all the operations had to be performed in the dark. Until a door could be found for use as an operating table, surgical operations were performed on the ground. Without the French and the Navy to help, it would have been impossible to move the wounded from the battlefield.

Despite the best efforts of the Royal Navy the wounded then endured a terrible eight-day voyage to Scutari where, for those who survived, equally unspeakable conditions awaited them.

The British hospital at Scutari became synonymous with all that was wrong with the British Army during the period of the Crimean War. Situated opposite Constantinople and overlooking the Bosporus on the Asian shore, the huge yellow-brick building had originally been a Turkish army barracks before being handed over to the British. Although designed to accommodate 2,000 soldiers, at the height of the war some 20,000 sick and wounded were packed into its overflowing corridors and rooms. When viewed from a distance the hospital was an imposing building, being four storeys high and built around a quadrangle with an imposing tower on each corner. Closer inspection revealed just how rundown it had become, with broken paving, dampness and filth from inadequate and blocked drains and sewers; worse, the hospital was infested with rats and vermin and it was about the last place suitable for accommodating seriously sick and wounded soldiers.

Even the landing stage was so dilapidated that ships could only disembark the sick in dinghies, another agonizing process for the suffering wounded. Those that survived this far were then conveyed on stretchers up the slope to the rapidly filling hospital. Thomas Chenery, *The Times* correspondent in Constantinople, was the first to report the shortcomings of the medical services when he wrote as early as 25 September 1854:

By the way, there is one experiment which has been a perfect failure. At the commencement of this war a plan was invented, and carried out, by which a number of Chelsea pensioners were sent out as an ambulancing corps to attend on the sick (the Hospital Conveyance Corps). Whether it was a scheme for saving money by utilizing the poor old men or shortening the duration of their lives and pensions, it is difficult to say, but they have been found in practice rather to require nurses themselves than to be able to nurse others. At Gallipoli and Bulgaria they died in numbers, while the whole of them are so weak as to be unable to perform the most ordinary duties. The man who conceived the idea that the hard work of a military hospital could be performed by worn-out and aged cripples must have had slight knowledge of warfare or have profited little by experience. To attend the sick who lie by hundreds in the wards of a vast hospital, and require unceasing care by night and day, is no easy task, and certainly cannot be performed by such old men as may be seen at Scutari – the remains of the body who were sent out six months ago. The soldiers attend upon each other, and directly a man is able to walk he is made useful in nursing his less advanced comrades, but the few pensioners are not of the slightest use.

The more he learned of the situation at Scutari, the more scathing Chenery's reports became. He followed up a few days later with another report that read:

It is with feelings of surprise and anger that the public will learn that no sufficient preparations have been made for the cure of the wounded. Not only are there not sufficient surgeons . . . not only are there no dressers and nurses . . . but what will be said when it is known that there is not even linen to make bandages for the wounded.

At that time the Army Medical Department had just 163 surgeons for the whole of the British Army and most of these were old men on half-pay. Chenery continued, incredulous that the British had been so ill prepared:

Can it be said that the battle of the Alma has been an event to take the world by surprise? Has not the expedition to the Crimea been the talk of the last four months? And when the Turks gave up to our use the vast barracks to form a hospital and depot, was it not on the ground that the loss of the English troops was sure to be considerable? And yet after the troops have been in the country there is no preparation for the commonest surgical operation.

Not only are the men kept, in some cases, for a week

7

without the hand of a medical man coming near their wounds – not only are they left to expire in agony, unheeded and shaken off, though catching desperately at the surgeon whenever he makes his rounds through the fetid ships, but now, when they are placed in the spacious building where we were led to believe that everything was ready which could ease their pain and facilitate their recovery, it is found that the commonest appliances of a workhouse sick ward are wanting and that the men must die through the medical staff of the British Army having forgotten that old rags are necessary for the dressing of wounds.

The sick and wounded soldiers from the battlefields of Alma, Balaklava and Sebastopol had died in their thousands, in great pain, misery and terrible conditions, simply for want of care. It was the harrowing reports from the war correspondents William Russell and Thomas Chenery of *The Times* and Edwin Godkin of the *London Daily News,* writing about the desperate plight of the sick and wounded soldiers and appalling conditions at the main British hospital at Scutari, that outraged the unsuspecting British public. *The Times* swiftly launched an appeal for which £20,000 was raised, well above all expectations. Prompted by this publicity, a single-minded nursing superintendent named Florence Nightingale volunteered her services and, using her influential contacts, was given official support to take a group of nurses to work in the military hospitals of British occupied Turkey.

Florence Nightingale was a nursing superintendent at a time when the profession was not well respected. She had been inspired by an experiment at Kaiserswerth in Germany where the Protestant Deaconesses' Movement had set up a model hospital that not only attended the sick but also trained 'well-bred and educated young women to become nurses'. The Nightingale family was well connected and Florence was friendly with Sydney Herbert, who was Secretary of War in charge of finances. Herbert had long been interested in the care of the sick and *The Times* campaign prompted him to write to his friend, Florence Nightingale:

There is but one person in England that I know of who would be capable of organizing and superintending such a scheme . . .

The selection of the rank and file of nurses will be very difficult: no one knows it better than yourself. The difficulty of finding women equal to the task, after all, full of horrors, and requiring, besides knowledge and goodwill, great energy and great courage, will be great . . . .

My question simply is, would you listen to the request to go and superintend the whole thing?

Herbert gained the approval of the government to support such an enterprise and with official backing, Miss Florence Nightingale set about recruiting her staff. The party consisted of fourteen hospital nurses and twenty-four nuns and Anglican sisters, who were dressed in a uniform of grey tweed with short red woollen capes. A scarf with 'Scutari' embroidered in red was draped over the shoulders.

On 21 October 1854, just a fortnight after Chenery's reports had appeared in *The Times*, the band of volunteer nurses left London. Two weeks later they spotted the minarets of Constantinople through a misty rain. When they landed at Scutari, Miss Nightingale sent ten of her nurses to the smaller, but marginally better maintained, neighbouring hospitals. She then took the remainder into the British hospital just as the wounded remnants of the Light Brigade, which had made their famous but disastrous charge against the Russian guns at Balaklava, were being received.

Although she and her staff were ready to go to work, Miss Nightingale would not allow their participation until the doctors specifically asked her. This was to convince the sceptical authorities that the nurses were not a reforming band of females trying to prove the incompetence of the male surgeons, but were present only to assist. So for a week or so, they sat in their cramped quarters in one of the corner towers, and rolled bandages. Such was the number of admissions that the doctors had to swallow their pride and belatedly request the nurses to help.

Miss Nightingale later recalled that she did not leave the

hospital for ten days. As anticipated, she found conditions there appalling with even the most basic of essentials absent and, to anyone less single-minded, the problems seemed insurmountable. The priority was to clean the filthy wards and corridors and to this end she requisitioned 300 scrubbing brushes and, in a short time, made the wards clean and free of vermin. This cleaning began a momentum that did not cease. Another essential was to clear the drains and sewers so the all-pervading stench was lessened. It took the Government's new inspectorate, the Sanitary Commission, to actually eradicate this principal source of infection.

Florence Nightingale ordered such basic items as linen for bandages, plates, cutlery, trays, beds, chairs, stools, blankets, mops, brooms, bowls, towels, scissors, disinfecting fluid, nightshirts and lanterns. Her direct line to Sydney Herbert cut through all military red tape and urgent medical supplies soon began to arrive. This contrasted with the bureaucratic procedures that existed in the Army's own Medical Department; if an Army doctor wanted to requisition anything, his request had to pass through a labyrinth of departments until it was lost or languished for want of another signature. After a while it dawned on the frustrated doctors that there was only one person in the hospital that was able to circumvent the stifling bureaucracy, and, more importantly, had the money to supply all their needs. In the end, the surgeons made their requests to Miss Nightingale for they knew that she was able to obtain anything that was required.

There was little Miss Nightingale could do about the overcrowding at Scutari and it was estimated that there were four miles of patients with barely eighteen inches between them. Her small staff was augmented by the arrival of another batch of forty-seven volunteer nurses and she was able to increase Scutari to fifty nurses and place the others in the smaller hospitals that had sprung up around the area. She also found a use for the 200 female camp followers, who had been abandoned when the regiments had crossed the Black Sea. A nearby house was rented, boilers installed and the soldiers' wives were employed as laundresses, so the hospital had a constant supply of clean linen. Using *The Times* fund, she provided proper bedding, clothing and 'comforts' and soon the nurses brought order to the chaos, and cleanliness to the confusion and filth, that had gripped the hospital.

Miss Nightingale also turned her attention to proper and well-prepared food and had three 'Extra Diet Kitchens' installed. Instead of the previous meals of inedible meat cooked in one kitchen so that when it was served to the patient it was cold, a proper invalid diet of arrowroot, sago, rice pudding, beef tea and lemonade was administered. In 1855 the celebrated chef, Alexis Soyer, arrived and organized the British hospital kitchen. He was the chef at the Reform Club and had been previously employed by the Duke of Sutherland. He soon became another active figure in the Red Cross movement. Conditions during Miss Nightingale's regime improved dramatically. Of the 16,297 soldiers who died of disease and neglect, 13,150 perished during the first nine months of the war before her methods had become established. By the end of the war, she had control of 125 nurses and it is not overstating her achievement to say that Florence Nightingale made the authorities recognize the part that nurses could play in military hospitals.

She and her staff generally and successfully won over the hostility they initially encountered from the Army doctors who had resented their presence as being a slur on their profession. They nicknamed her 'The Bird'. Instead of confrontation when the military made things difficult for her and her staff, Miss Nightingale chose to cooperate and to show, by example, how to make life easier for everyone.

Although they were not involved in medical duties, the efforts of the nurses dramatically reduced the mortality rate. There can be little doubt that the Crimean War was the cradle of modern nursing and changed the face of military nursing for men, and especially women, forever. Before Florence Nightingale and her volunteers had arrived, admission to Scutari Hospital was akin to a death sentence to those unfortunate enough to be sent there. News of the dramatic changes she had brought about soon reached the outside world, news that ensured she became an international heroine.

Florence Nightingale almost single-handedly removed the

stigma of being a nurse. The profession, if it could have been so graced, had previously attracted mostly unsavoury and uncaring women, often alcoholics or worse, which contributed to the low public opinion of hospitals. On her return from the Crimea, and riding on a wave of popular support and interest, Florence Nightingale set about putting nursing on a professional footing by establishing strict codes and high standards that would attract more suitable candidates.

Despite the success of Florence Nightingale's nursing staff in the Crimea, there were mixed reactions to the continuing employment of women as military nurses and it was not until the draft *Regulations for the Inspector General of Hospitals* was published in 1857 that any effort was made to employ women, but it took six years for the first woman to appear in the British Army list, when Jane Shaw Stewart was appointed Superintendent General of Female Nurses at the general hospital at the Army Training School for military nurses at the Royal Victoria Hospital, Netley in 1863. Mrs Stewart resigned in 1868 and was replaced by Mrs Deeble, the widow of an Army surgeon who, in 1879, took six nurses from Netley to South Africa to assist with the wounded from the Anglo Zulu War.

In keeping with the age, religion played a significant role in the nursing ethos. Several Catholic orders had been active and the Protestants were also anxious to become equally established. A Lutheran clergyman named Theodor Fliedner used the Deaconess movement at Kaiserswerth in Germany as a basis to found the first hospital that combined treatment of the sick with the training of nurses. This proved so successful that the Deaconess experiment was repeated in London where the German Hospital, and then Dr Laseron's Teaching Hospital at Tottenham, were established (the latter became The Prince of Wales' General Hospital).

Another important milestone in the establishment and acceptance of the nursing profession was the founding of the Red Cross in 1864. Its founder, a Swiss named Henri Dunant, had witnessed the Battle of Solferino in northern Italy in 1859 and had been so moved by the unimaginable sufferings of the wounded that he resolved that men injured in the service of their country, no matter on which side, should have proper medical and nursing care. The international community quickly embraced this concept in principle but little was actually put into effect until the Franco-Prussian War of 1870–71.

When the Franco-Prussian War broke out in the summer of 1870, John Furley, a young London solicitor and keen advocate of the Red Cross ideal, persuaded a retired Army officer named Colonel Robert Loyd-Lindsay VC to use his name and influence to launch a British society. Loyd-Lindsay was a well-known and respected war hero who, for gallantry in the Crimean War, was one of the first recipients of the Victoria Cross; he also subscribed to the Red Cross concept. Florence Nightingale was at first opposed to the idea of Red Cross societies becoming involved in wars for she held the view that they would, 'diminish the responsibility of each belligerent for its own sick and wounded.' Despite Florence Nightingale's mildly dismissive attitude, support in the form of money and volunteers poured into the 'Society for Aiding and Ameliorating the Condition of the Sick and Wounded in Times of War'. This title was soon changed to the more manageable 'British Aid Society' with Queen Victoria as its patron and the Prince of Wales as president. This was the beginning of an unbroken royal link with the British Red Cross. The Society first proved its worth during the Franco-Prussian War of 1870–71; the precedent of the multi-national Red Cross had been established and it thereafter became a feature in future wars.

Chapter Two

Northern Italy 1859;
The Battle of Solferino

No quarter is given, it is sheer butchery . . . .
And no doctors or nurses to help the wounded
. . . only occasional passing tourists

After Florence Nightingale, the second person to have a profound effect on the young Janet Wells was Jean Henri Dunant.

A major advance in the care of sick and wounded soldiers occurred as a result of a chance visit to a battlefield by Dunant, not with the plight of the casualties in mind, but while trying to gain support for a commercial enterprise in North Africa from the French Emperor, Napoleon III. In 1859, the year of Janet Well's birth, Dunant was desperate to salvage his dream of turning an area of Algeria into a well-watered and fertile breadbasket for Europe. He had even written a book about his ambitious ideas for land development in north Africa entitled *Memorandum on the Financial and Industrial Company of the Mons-Gemila Mills in Algeria.* Now, rather unsurprisingly, a lack of water was threatening the whole enterprise and Dunant was desperate to secure the concessions in Algeria, that he felt would save his investment, from the Emperor. He devised a convoluted plan based on flattery. He wrote a book in which he showed a direct link of succession from Charlemagne to the Napoleons. This he had beautifully bound and was confident that Napoleon would grant him an audience and be amenable to his request for help in Algeria.

14

Dunant's timing was unfortunate as the neighbouring Austrian Empire was already beginning its slow decline and was bedevilled by unrest in many of her diverse provinces. In particular, Austria was desperate to hang on to her subject states in Hungary and northern Italy. When the independent state of Piedmont, under the leadership of Garibaldi and Cavour, began to ferment nationalistic yearnings in neighbouring Lombardy, Austria declared war and invaded Piedmont. The French, under the bombastic Napoleon III, sided with the Piedmontese and in May joined forces with the Italians to push the Austrians out of both Lombardy and Venetia and, for a few short weeks, the Lombardy plain became a bloody battleground.

With Napoleon III taking overall command, Dunant seized the opportunity to approach the Emperor while he was on campaign and away from all the obstacles of the Parisian court. Dressed in an immaculate white tropical suit, Dunant crossed the Alps and visited a friend, General de Beaufort, Chief of Staff to Prince Jérôme Napoleon, who gave him a letter of recommendation. De Beaufort also advised Dunant that if he wanted to watch a first-class battle, he should travel at once to Castiglione, where the French army was concentrating.

The Franco-Italian army had quickly ejected the Austrians from Piedmont and followed up with major successes on 27 May near Montebello and the bigger confrontation on 4 June at Magenta. The Austrians fell back and fortified a fifteen mile long line of low hills running north to south between Pozzolengo, Solferino, Cavriano and Guidizzolo. The Austrian army was formidable, consisting of 170,000 men and 500 guns; while the armies knew there was to be a battle, the timing of their confrontation took them equally unawares. With little reconnaissance or intelligence gathering by either side, the two armies met at daybreak on Midsummer's Day, 24 June. The first shots heralded a battle that was to last for fifteen hours. With Napoleon commanding the allies and the young Franz-Josef leading the Austrians, this was the last occasion on which opposing armies were commanded by their respective monarchs. The start of the battle was as the painters of the day liked to portray combat, full of colour and panache. The massed blocks of white-clad

Austrians marched to the beat of drums beneath their yellow and black battle flags, emblazoned with the Imperial eagle. The bright blues, greens and reds of the French hussars could be seen as they picked their way through the maze of paths and vineyards that lay between the two adversaries. The brilliant sunlight reflected off the cuirasses of the French dragoons and from the lance tips of the lancers. The air was filled with the cacophony of jangling horses, creaking wagons, tramping infantry, shouted commands and the blowing of bugles. With so many men and horses in motion, a huge pall of dust was raised that soon dulled the splendour of the two armies.

Both sides had been thrown into the fight after exhaustive night marches and neither side had had time to eat. By midday, the temperatures had soared; the soldiers became dehydrated and weak from hunger and fatigue. The artillery from both sides was causing huge numbers of casualties as the battle became a slugging match. The main action was centred on Solferino with its tall tower known to the soldiers as 'Italy's Spy'. This changed hands several times during the day and 6,000 soldiers lost their lives in their struggle to gain control of the town.

Dunant later wrote:

Compact columns of men throw themselves upon each other with an impetuosity of a destructive torrent that carries everything before it.

Every mound, every height, every rocky crag, is the scene of a fight to the death; bodies lie in heaps on the hills and in the valleys . . . Here is a hand-to-hand struggle in all its horror and frightfulness; Austrian and Allies trampling each other under foot, killing one another on piles of bleeding corpses, felling their enemies with rifle butts, crushing skulls, ripping bellies open with sabre and bayonet. No quarter is given, it is sheer butchery; a struggle between savage beasts, maddened with blood and fury . . . Wounded and dead are ridden over by cavalry and horse artillery.

During the afternoon, the more mobile French began to gain the upper hand over the ponderous massed ranks of Austrian

16

infantry. Both sides had fought each other almost to a standstill and it took a change in the weather to finally decide the outcome. About 4 p.m., the relentless sun disappeared as black clouds darkened the battlefield and a strong wind began to gust, which threw up blinding, choking dust to add to the soldiers' misery. As dusk approached, thunder and lightning accompanied a torrential downpour of hail and rain that effectively signalled the end of the battle as the Austrians retreated. The storm saturated the countryside and traffic on the dirt roads quickly turned them into a quagmire. This made access virtually impossible to the 30,000 wounded who were scattered about for miles and the few horse or ox drawn cart ambulances in service were unable to make progress. The only form of relief was the few remaining *cantinières*, the French women who accompanied their husbands' regiments with their small barrels of brandy. It was another twelve hours before the ground had dried sufficiently to enable the wounded to be collected.

Dunant arrived at the small town of Castiglione as a constant stream of walking-wounded was filling up the small town, but it was not until daybreak the following day that he was able to see the scenes of utter destruction covering the plain below. Ruined villages, vineyards and orchards destroyed, and everywhere lay dead and dying men. He later wrote:

> Bodies of men and horses covered the battlefield; corpses were strewn over roads, ditches, ravines, thickets and fields; the approaches to Solferino were literally thick with dead. The fields were devastated, wheat and corn lying flat on the ground, fences broken, orchards ruined; here and there were pools of blood . . . All around Solferino, and especially in the village cemetery, the ground was littered with guns, knapsacks, cartridge boxes, mess tins, helmets, shakoes, fatigue caps, bells, equipment of every kind, remnants of blood-stained clothing and piles of broken weapons.

Dunant picked his way amongst this scene of utter destruction and was continually struck by the need to do something to relieve the terrible suffering he saw all around him:

The poor wounded men . . . were ghastly pale and exhausted. Some, who had been most badly hurt, had a stupefied look. Some were anxious and excited by nervous strain and shaken by spasmodic trembling. Some, who had gaping wounds already beginning to show infection, were almost crazed with suffering. They begged to be put out of their misery; and writhed with faces distorted in the grip of the death struggle . . . Many were disfigured . . . their limbs stiffened, their bodies blotched with ghastly spots, their hands clawing at the ground, their eyes staring wildly, their moustaches bristling.

It soon became clear that there was no one either collecting or going to the aid of these poor wretches. Returning to Castiglione he set about organizing the village women to take food and water to the wounded and, wherever possible, to bring in the less hopeless cases. He later remarked on how impressed and moved he had been by the attitude of these simple peasant women who were willing to help all wounded irrespective of their nationality; they described their actions with the words *Tutti Fratelli* (We are all brothers). Unfortunately, not all the peasants subscribed to this philosophy of brotherhood and the battlefield was a target for scavenging locals who, without any conscience, robbed the dead and wounded alike.

Dunant found one German and four Austrian doctors among the prisoners and set them to work in the church at San Maggiore, already filled with 500 wounded from both sides. All available linen and lint was collected and teams of helpers were assigned to bandage wounds.

On 27 June Dunant sent his coachman to nearby Brescia with a shopping list for camomile, mallows, elder flowers, oranges, lemons, sugar, sponges, bandages, pins, shirts and 'comforts' such as cigars and tobacco. Among the extra helpers he managed to enlist were four English tourists, a retired naval officer, an Italian priest, a Parisian journalist and a chocolate manufacturer from Neuchâtel named Philippe Suchard. Dunant set them to work dressing wounds, carrying messages and writing letters for the patients. For some of these enlisted civilians though, the sights and smells were too much for ordinary people to endure and they soon quit.

Castiglione now held over 10,000 sick and wounded, many of whom were still awaiting attention four days after the battle. The few doctors present were completely exhausted and it was recorded that one surgeon was only able to continue operating because two assistants held up his arms. On one occasion, Dunant returned to San Maggiore to find that some Italian soldiers had dragged out a couple of wounded Austrian prisoners and were about to throw them down the steps. Dunant intervened with a plea to stop and echoed the words of the peasant women that soon became a watchword, *Tutti Fratelli!*

With his white, but by now grubby, suit, Henri Dunant had become a 'Nightingale' figure amongst the wounded and was soon known as 'The Man in White'. He later wrote:

If an international relief society had existed at the time of Solferino and if there had been volunteer helpers at Castiglione on 24–26th June or at Brescia at about the same time, as well as Mantua or Verona, what endless good they could have done!

Late on the 27th he left Castiglione to visit General MacMahon to describe the plight of the wounded and to persuade the French to release and use the captured Austrian doctors. Briefly returning to Castiglione, Dunant continued to Brescia where the majority of wounded were being treated. He found two churches full of wounded soldiers that appeared more in need of his assistance than others. He again sought help from passing tourists, including some English, and from the less seriously wounded patients.

With medical supplies no more readily available than before, Dunant toured the makeshift hospitals, giving out tobacco and pipes and writing letters. He later reflected:

How valuable it would have been in those Lombardy towns to have had a hundred experienced and qualified orderlies and nurses! Such a group would have formed a nucleus

19

around which could have been rallied the scanty help and dispersed efforts which needed competent guidance. As it was, there was no time for those who knew their business to give the needful advice and guidance, and most of those who brought their own goodwill to the task lacked the necessary knowledge and experience, so that their efforts were inadequate and often ineffective.

There is little doubt he was talking about himself and expressing his frustration at not being able to do more. Dunant felt both physically and mentally drained and unable to be of any more practical assistance. He then travelled to Milan, where he first touched on the idea that doctors and hospitals should bear some sign or symbol that would be respected by all sides but his suggestion was regarded as wishful thinking and impractical. Here he remained until the war ended in July. It was with a sense of relief that he returned to the fresh alpine air of Switzerland to try and salvage his interrupted business ventures.

Napoleon had initially sent a telegram to his wife, Eugenie, crowing of a great victory. When he realized the extent of the carnage at Solferino he was so shocked that he feared there would be further excessive bloodshed if he attacked the Austrian fortresses of the Quadrilateral, which blocked the route to Venetia.

Uncharacteristically for such a vainglorious man, he chose to abandon the war and signed the Truce of Villafranca. Instead, it was left to Garibaldi and Cavour to complete the Risorgimento, the unification of Italy, during the following decade.

CHAPTER THREE

Founding of the Red Cross

A time of terrible war, not much medicine and no nurses . . .

Jean Henri Dunant was a caring and sensitive man and the memories of the past three months weighed heavily upon him. Without doubt, he suffered a nervous breakdown and had to spend several weeks recuperating in the mountains until he felt well enough to tackle his tangled business affairs. His unsolicited humanitarian efforts in the face of the almost total breakdown in the French army medical organization went unrecognized until King Victor Emmanuel acknowledged Dunant's work among the wounded; in January 1860, he presented him with the Order of Saint Maurice and Saint Lazarus of Italy.

This did little to compensate for the business worries and the continuing trauma of Solferino haunted the highly-strung young Swiss. His increasing irritability and tantrums alienated his family and, in early 1861, he moved out of the family home into a small rented room. Alone and haunted by his memories of terrible war, and not much medicine and no nurses, Dunant began to write about his thoughts and experiences, more as a cathartic exercise than an attempt at literature. He wrote:

> I was, as it were, lifted out of myself, compelled by some higher power and inspired by the breath of God. In this state of pent-up emotion which filled my heart, I was aware of an intuition, vague and yet profound, that my work was an instrument of His Will, it seemed to me that it was destined

to have fruits of infinite consequence for mankind. This presentiment drove me on and I had the sensation of being urged by a force beyond myself.

Writing with passion, his account was not just another report about a battle but championed the revolutionary idea of a neutral, inviolate medical organization to care for the sick and wounded of all sides:

Would it not be possible, in time of peace and quiet, to form relief societies for the purpose of having care given to the wounded in wartime by zealous, devoted, and thoroughly qualified volunteers?

By October 1862, he had completed his manuscript, which he entitled *A Memory of Solferino*. The writing experience had been a sufficiently therapeutic one and a revived Dunant was keen to share his message but modestly ordered just 1,600 copies to be printed for distribution amongst friends, acquaintances and local dignitaries. The reaction was astonishing. The book became an instant talking point and two more printings quickly followed to meet the demand.

One of the first people to read *A Memory of Solferino* was a lawyer named Gustav Moynier, who was president of the Genevese *Société d'Utilité Publique*. Moved by the description of the suffering and Dunant's revolutionary idea of a neutral volunteer medical corps, Moynier paid Dunant a visit. As a result, Dunant and Moynier formed a working group called the 'International Committee for the Relief to the Wounded'.

It was essential to have *A Memory of Solferino* translated into the major languages and distributed throughout Europe, with particular targets being the crowned heads and medical establishments. Dunant travelled to conferences around the Continent where he delivered persuasive speeches and successfully lobbied for support. Prussia and other German principalities were among the first to wholeheartedly embrace this new concept.

Soon, individual countries had formed their own committees subscribing to Dunant's philosophy and the concept gathered momentum. It was decided in October 1863, just a year after Dunant's book had been finished, that all neutral volunteers should wear some distinctive sign to protect them on the battle-field. It was a Dr Appia who came up with the suggestion of a white armband with a red cross in the middle – the reverse of the Swiss national flag – and an icon was born.

While the Red Cross, as the society had become known, grad-ually expanded and flourished, Dunant's business did the reverse. Dunant was leading a double life; he was fêted by royalty throughout Europe, treated with great respect by government leaders and praised by his peers. Victor Hugo told him; 'You armed humanity and served liberty' while Charles Dickens wrote an essay in praise of 'The Man in White'. At a time when he should have been savouring his well-deserved fame, Dunant was slipping deeper into debt. An official report went so far as to accuse him of being dishonest and immoral. This, and the fact that many of his friends had lost money due to his poor business acumen, caused Dunant to leave Geneva forever and to resign from his brainchild, the Red Cross.

After reading *A Memory of Solferino* Gustav Moynier wrote:

The author of this book opened the eyes of the blind, moved the hearts of the indifferent and virtually affected in the intellectual and moral realm the reformation to which it aspired, in such a manner that after this first conquest was once gained, nothing remained than to give it concrete form.

True, Moynier did give Dunant's dream concrete form, but he was jealous of Dunant's fame, which he felt was unwarranted. When Dunant became bankrupt, humiliated and exiled, Moynier started his campaign to rewrite history culminating in his biography in which he managed to trace the origins of the Red Cross movement without even mentioning Henri Dunant. Lacking both money and determination, Dunant lived in Paris in genteel squalor, sustained only by handouts from friends and admirers. His old vigour briefly flickered during the Siege of Paris when he worked with the French Red Cross, collecting clothing and visiting the wounded. After the war, Dunant co-founded the Universal Alliance for Order and Civilization along with such men as Ferdinand de Lesseps and Frédéric Passy. Dunant was to share the inaugural Nobel Peace Prize in 1901 with Passy. He did not touch any of the prize money but left the proceeds in his will to those investors who had lost money in his earlier ventures. He died in 1910 at the age of eighty-two. His Red Cross had concerned itself with trying to bring about an international law on the treatment of prisoners, which appeared to be heading for general acceptance (though it was not until 1929 that the Geneva Convention on the treatment of prisoners of war finally came into force).

In Britain, meanwhile, the organization which evolved into the familiar British Red Cross Society, received a particularly welcome endorsement from the usually hypercritical Florence Nightingale.

The day the Society was founded, 4 August 1870, was also the first day of the battle between the Prussians and French at Worth in Germany. That evening, John Furley, now a British Red Cross representative, left London to visit Paris and then Berlin to meet the French and German Red Cross Presidents respectively and to find how the new British Society could be of help. In Geneva, he met with Gustav Moynier, who was excited at the prospect of seeing all his fine ideas put to the test in the Red Cross's first conflict. After a hectic ten days, he returned to London to find the public response to the formation of the Society had been overwhelming. Literally so, for extra premises had to be rented to accommodate the gifts and donations that poured in. By the end of August, the fund held £30,000 and by the end of the short-lived war the British public had subscribed an incredible £294,000, a huge fortune in Victorian times.

British volunteer doctors had also been sent to help at the many field hospitals that sprang up along the line of the Prussian advance. Furley then set out on a long trip, visiting the sick and wounded on both sides, distributing medical supplies and comforts. When these ran out, he crossed the border into Luxembourg and bought more. He travelled through a devastated landscape, littered with burned out farms, villages reduced to rubble and everywhere the debris of war – the rotting carcasses of horses, smashed wagons, discarded helmets and associated military accoutrements. He found the French were suspicious of any foreigner, seeing spies everywhere and not trusting the Red Cross's neutral stance. Pierre Boissier, whose family's association with the Red Cross goes back to its inception, wrote in his book, *From Solferino to Tsushima*:

> Above all, it was France's own wounded who suffered the most from neglect of the advantages offered by the (Red Cross) Convention.

On numerous occasions, the French tried to evacuate field hospitals. Hurriedly crammed into makeshift vehicles, suffering agonies at each jolt on the way, the wounded remained for days without receiving any treatment whatsoever. Hundreds of the wounded died during these murderous convoys of hopelessly entangled ammunition wagons and columns of troops clogging the roads. Many of them could have been saved if, despite the Prussian advance, the hospital had remained in the field with all its personnel. Furley was later followed by other committee members leading teams of doctors and nurses. A British team witnessed the Battle of Sedan, in which Napoleon surrendered and 80,000 French soldiers went into captivity. The enormous numbers of wounded from both sides kept all medical staff working without a break. For the first time in a report to the Society, written by Dr M. Sims, special reference was made to the use of female nurses:

> As nurses, I would not exchange one woman for a dozen men. From the moment that women were introduced as nurses, the whole aspect of our establishment was changed.

Sims seems to have been in a minority, for the general opinion of the male medical volunteers was that although the Nightingale-trained nurses were tolerated, female volunteers were held in contempt. It appeared that women, even those who were trained, still had a long way to go to be accepted in a theatre of war.

The war was finally concluded in early 1871 and the British

Committee distributed the last of its supplies before returning home. They had sound reason to feel satisfied as they had started from scratch and in a very short time evolved into the most effective and widespread of the many foreign volunteer services that had responded to the humanitarian call. Although many of the members had experience, both military and medical, and were thus prepared for the sights they met, most of the volunteers were civilians. They had to come to terms with the sight of what modern weapons could do to the human body, the devastation of whole towns and the dead-eyed hopelessness of dispossessed people. They saw hunger that reduced starving soldiers and civilians to eat the rotting entrails of dead horses and smelt the nauseous smell of men dying of disease and gangrene. It was a very steep learning curve for this new breed of volunteer and one that most passed with flying colours.

CHAPTER FOUR

1859 . . . The age of pox and plagues . . . and wars

W hen Janet Wells was born, England was under the firm rule of Queen Victoria, aided by her beloved Albert, the Prince Consort, whose strong support ensured that the Queen was a very effective monarch. Albert advised but never interfered.

These were exciting times. Although the Indian Mutiny rumbled on, it no longer commanded the public's interest once the mutineers were put to flight and routed by the British Army. The British Empire was steadily expanding and Britain's domination across the world spread like a pool of red ink across Queen Victoria's globe as her armies and administrators brought peace, order and control to the new colonies. At home, peace and prosperity pervaded the land. A Royal Wedding added to the on-going festive mood across the British Empire, when Queen Victoria's eldest daughter Victoria married Crown Prince Frederick William of Prussia, so beginning a series of marriages that linked the Royal Houses of Europe with the British throne. As if to illustrate Britain's confidence and supremacy in the world, the Prussian court gave way to Queen Victoria's insistence that the wedding should take place in London and not Berlin. The Queen observed:

Whatever may be the usual practice of Prussian princes, it is not everyday that one marries the eldest daughter of the Queen of England.

Queen Victoria and Prince Albert were also at the forefront of expansion in the world of music, literature and art. The Queen was an accomplished artist and several books of her watercolours were published. The Prince was a noted flautist and classical musician and he and Victoria enjoyed plays, musicals and popular monologues, often arranging private performances at Windsor where the Prince regularly accompanied another accomplished flautist, Janet Well's father, Professor Benjamin Wells. Victoria also took a keen interest in the day-to-day administration of her country. Wherever the pair worked, Prince Albert had a desk alongside that of his wife, and to acknowledge his status, his desk was positioned one inch lower than that of his wife.

The ever-fragile relationship between Britain and France continued to bounce along, yet the underlying tension between the two countries did not deter English ladies from enthusiastically embracing the latest outrageous Parisian fashion, the crinoline, as favoured by the flamboyant Empress Eugenie of France. This fashion was the last throw of extravagance and excess before Britain would descend into stern faced respectability led by a mourning Queen. Among those who railed against the crinoline was the most famous woman of the age, Florence Nightingale. Riding on the crest of popularity after the Crimean War, the 'Lady with the Lamp' was working hard to organize nursing into a worthwhile profession by setting teaching guidelines and attracting a better-educated class of candidates. In her *Nursing Handbook*, she devoted nearly a page to the evils of wearing a crinoline, opining that:

> I wish too that people who wear a crinoline could see the indecency of their own dress as other people see it. A respectable elderly woman stooping forward, invested in crinoline, exposes quite as much of her person to the patient lying in the room as any opera dancer does on the stage. But no one will tell her this unpleasant truth.

The fidget of silk and of the crinoline, the crackling of starched petticoats, the rattling of keys, the creaking of stays and of shoes, will do a patient more harm than all the medicines in the world will do him good.

As the country prospered from the wealth of trade with the empire, new inventions came thick and fast. Britain's businesses were expanding rapidly and many of the rural poor could now find work and affordable housing in the rapidly developing industries of the growing towns and cities. It was not, however, a totally rosy picture. British society was one of opposite extremes. The rapid expansion of industry meant that large tracts of land were covered with factories and workshops. These working hubs quickly became surrounded by streets of tightly packed small cheap houses for the new workforce. Great wealth sat beside severe poverty as the newly-rich built themselves magnificent houses and estates; the employment of staff to service these establishments created not only work but also a new hierarchy of domestic servants.

With the migration of the working population towards densely packed towns it was fortunate that developments in medicine and surgery were also rapidly expanding. Such famous men as William Little, who established the first orthopaedic hospital in London in 1840, and Hugh Owen Thomas, responsible for introducing splints for fractures and other instruments for correcting limb deformities, greatly advanced trauma surgery. Lord Joseph Lister became famous for introducing antiseptic surgery, which reduced the mortality rate of all operations. His antiseptic dressings were a lifesaver to patients by preventing sepsis of the wound which, without antibiotics, was seriously life threatening.

Surgery, whilst based on improving knowledge of human anatomy, was limited by terrible difficulties in the early nineteenth century. Anaesthetics were not used to relieve pain in surgery until the 1840s, so operations had to be performed quickly. Rapid progress was made only when a Professor of Midwifery at Edinburgh University decided to experiment with a new anaesthetic called chloroform, using it to reduce the pain women had to go through when giving birth. He had previously used a chemical called ether, which made patients cough, unlike chloroform. Within a month he had successfully used it on over fifty patients and the first operation conducted under chloroform at the London Hospital took place in February 1847.

The use of anaesthesia in surgery was found to reduce operative shock; it eliminated pain and enabled longer and more complicated surgery to be undertaken. The surgeon's greatest handicap was his unwitting ignorance of germs and infection which frequently caused wounds to become infected. Unsterilized surgical instruments spread germs and though many patients survived an operation there was the probability they would then die of blood poisoning.

By 1859 anaesthetics in surgery and obstetrics had become widespread and chloroform received Royal approval when Queen Victoria had it administered during her eighth confinement, though only five years earlier, in 1854, the Inspector General of Hospitals, Dr John Hall, issued a memorandum to surgeons serving in the Crimean War in which he stated that:

> ... however barbarous it may appear, the smart of the knife is a powerful stimulant; and it is better to hear a man bawl lustily, than to see him sink silently into the grave.

During this period there was a massive expansion in the number of hospitals in Britain and these establishments were the focus of nationwide health care and medical education. Yet despite the growing role of hospitals, there were wide variations in the quality of medical services available. They ranged from voluntary general hospitals, a few celebrated specialist hospitals served by famous surgeons, through to the appalling workhouse infirmaries where untrained nurses looked after pauper patients. Voluntary hospitals, which were philanthropic charitable institutions, were initially intended to serve the poor without charge; the majority were built in the period 1750 to 1800 and by the 1850s they were an established feature of most towns. Funded from subscriptions and donations, many charitable fundraising and social events were held to support such local hospitals. Fairs, dances, teas and sales became a focus of entertainment for the community. Most general voluntary hospitals excluded certain categories of patients; as a consequence ancillary hospitals were founded to deal with neglected groups of patients and the less glamorous areas of medicine. Sometimes, relatives of those who had been touched by an uncommon or difficult-to-treat disease started a specialist hospital in order to improve understanding and treatment of the condition. More often, entrepreneurial doctors with an interest in a particular condition founded their own hospital due to the difficulty in advancing their careers within a general hospital. This also gave them the opportunity to study more examples of any single disease than would be found at a general hospital.

Before the 1850s nurses, whether employed privately or in hospitals, were usually uneducated and formal training was rare. Some attempts had been made to improve the situation and a number of nursing sisterhoods were founded in emulation of the developing European system of Catholic nursing schools. The most notable progress in England came when the Florence Nightingale School was established at St Thomas's Hospital in 1860. In that year there were sixty-six special hospitals and dispensaries in London alone; some dealt with particular diseases or parts of the body, others with particular age groups. Cancer was rarely treated in general hospitals but within specialist institutions, while mineral water and sea-bathing hospitals specialized in the treatment of arthritis, rheumatism, gout, paralysis and skin complaints. There were eye hospitals, ear, nose and throat hospitals, children's hospitals, and hospitals for women. Very few women gave birth in hospital, but those who did attended lying-in hospitals. There were also orthopaedic hospitals for chronically disabled children, or 'cripples' as these unfortunates were commonly known. It was, however, considered extremely hazardous to be treated in any hospital, even the most famous teaching hospitals, as the mortality rate from infection was very high.

This situation was fully recognized, if not understood, by doctors and patients alike. Florence Nightingale, in *Notes on Hospitals*, in 1859, said:

It may seem a strange principle to enunciate as the very first requirement in a hospital that it should do the sick no harm. It is quite necessary nevertheless to lay down such a principle, because the actual mortality in hospitals, especially those of the crowded cities, is very much higher than any calculation founded on the mortality of the same class of patient treated out of hospital would lead us to expect.

There was a variety of contributory factors; artery forceps were not introduced to stop bleeding until the 1850s and surgeons relied on tourniquets (tight bands), cauteries (hot irons) and ligatures (silk threads) to prevent blood loss. In the 1870s surgeons began to appreciate the importance of hygiene and preventing germs in surgery by using antiseptics like carbolic acid.

Understandably, the majority of the well-off population preferred the more socially acceptable and safer tradition of being treated in their own homes. Some surgery was still carried out in the home and qualified nurses were sought to care for the patient as unqualified 'nurses' of dubious background and ability abounded. Among those able to pay for their care, a great deal of reliance was placed on the recommendation of the attending physician or surgeon, or on the certificate acquired by a nurse from a reputable or famous training hospital.

Yet many of the wealthy members of society were mindful of the plight of the working class and became great philanthropists. Charitable and religious organizations sprang up and did much to try to alleviate the suffering of the poor but it was the early projects into public health, enforced by the Public Health Acts of 1858 and 1859, which tentatively sought to involve local authorities in such schemes as adequate housing, clean water supplies and drainage. The government was only intermittently concerned with the population's welfare and it took a serious outbreak of cholera during the mid 1860s to pass the 1866 Public Health Act, which forced local authorities into action. Even then, progress was fatally slow and it was noted that in 1869 the supply of water to London, Birmingham and Manchester was of a quality that was publicly described as being '. . . a criminal indifference to the public safety' and at times the quality of drinking water and drainage was so poor that epidemics of typhoid, cholera and dysentery continued to be commonplace. Tuberculosis, caused by the cramped and unsanitary conditions of the poor and the infectious nature of the disease, was also endemic. Even smallpox was not unknown, though medical improvements and increased awareness for tackling the sources of the terrible epidemics that continued to ravage the world's leading power began to take effect.

Unsurprisingly, the late 1870s was known as the age of 'pox and plagues'. Humanity remained largely powerless to prevent disease until Louis Pasteur in France and Robert Koch in Germany developed conclusive proof of the germ theory. Their bacteriological findings eventually led to the first steps in the conquest of infectious diseases. At home, environmental sanitation, safe water supplies, improved sewage disposal systems, experiments with the pasteurization of milk and sanitary control of food supplies gradually resulted in the virtual disappearance of cholera and typhoid fever and a marked reduction in diarrhoea and infant mortality. The later discovery of effective vaccines, based on the growth of the science of micro-biology, initiated not only the eventual worldwide eradication of smallpox but also caused the marked decline in such common diseases as diphtheria, tetanus, whooping cough, poliomyelitis, and measles. Even so, according to *The Lancet*, UK civilian mortality rates in 1879 were still unacceptably high with 2.6 per cent of the population dying each winter month; London typi-cally suffered 189 deaths from smallpox alone in January. The infant mortality rate was 15.3 per cent (under twelve months old) compared with 0.6 per cent today. Life expectancy for the working classes in Rutland and Manchester (where detailed figures were maintained) were a mere thirty-eight years and twenty-six years respectively, and for the professional classes it was forty-two and fifty-two years respectively. With surgery in its infancy, the surgical death rate was nearly 25 per cent of all recorded surgical cases.

Whilst Florence Nightingale had little to do with the advances made in medicine, her influence in healthcare and hygiene was now legend. The fame her exploits had brought, enabled her to fulfil her ambition to set and control the standards for future generations of nurses through her training methods and writings. It was, especially, the magnificent work she did after the Crimean War, to improve the organization of care for the health of both the poor and the common soldier, that fascinated the young Janet Wells more than the romance of the 'Lady with the Lamp'. Janet avidly read Florence Nightingale's many books on nursing practices and training methods. She was greatly influenced by these writings and it was clear from an early stage which direction her life would take. Especially popular was the preface to Florence Nightingale's book *Notes on Nursing – what it is and what it is not* published six months before Miss Nightingale realized her ambition to establish her Training School for Nurses at St Thomas's Hospital in London.

The contents of these notes are practical, sensible and informative advice. The chapter, Health of Houses, illustrates her point about the appalling drainage in some houses by comparing them with her experience of the unsanitary drainage in Scutari Hospital. She stressed the importance of pure air, pure water, efficient drainage, cleanliness and light and observed that the close proximity of sick and injured patients in airless conditions caused the rapid spread of infection.

Like many others at this time, Florence believed that the 'foetid malodorous air' caused the spread of infection. Her designs for wards therefore were long, airy rooms with the beds down each side, set no less than eighteen inches apart. Each had an opening window above it so that the flow of air through the room was encouraged. Heating was provided by a cast iron or pot bellied stove at one end of the ward. This would be burnished to gleaming black spotlessness by one of the hapless probationer nurses.

Florence Nightingale wrote:

The following notes are by no means intended as a rule of thought by which nurses can teach themselves to nurse, still less as a manual to teach nurses to nurse. They are meant simply to give hints for thought to women who have personal charge of the health of others. Every woman, or at least almost every woman, in England, has at one time or another of her life, charge of the personal health of somebody, whether child or invalid, – in other words, every woman is a nurse. Every day sanitary knowledge, or the knowledge of nursing, or in other words, of how to put the constitution in such a state as that it will have no disease, or that it can recover from disease, takes a higher place. It is recognized as the knowledge which every one ought to have – distinct from medical knowledge, which only a profession can have.

If, then, every woman must at some time or other of her life, become a nurse, i.e. have charge of somebody's health, how immense and how valuable would be the produce of her united experience if every woman would think how to nurse.

I do not pretend to teach her how, I ask her to teach herself, and for this purpose I venture to give her some hints.

It was, without any doubt, Florence Nightingale's work and her prominent position in society that allowed nursing to become a profession suitable for young respectable Victorian women like Janet Wells. Because of her religious convictions, Florence Nightingale devoutly believed that nursing was an art that required vision and idealism, making it the most exalted of vocations. She believed it should be concerned with principles of character formation, efficient management, hygiene and sanitation, which required organized obedience and discipline.

PART II

Nurse Janet Wells

CHAPTER FIVE

If you must faint nurse . . .

do it backwards, away from the operating table . . .

It was into this dangerous but exciting world that Janet Helen Wells was born in 1859, the second child of five daughters and three sons, to Elizabeth and Benjamin Wells of Shepherd's Bush in west London.

Benjamin was a very talented musician and a professor of music. In his youth he had performed in a concert for the Duke of Wellington, where he impressed and was encouraged by Felix Mendelssohn. Benjamin became one of the foremost flautists of his generation and he often played for the rich and famous, becoming a firm favourite of the Royal Family. On several occasions he played by Royal Command at Windsor Castle, even playing duets with Prince Albert, who was an accomplished flautist. Benjamin also liked to write entertaining tales about flute playing, in the form of long verses typical of the Victorian era and anyone who excelled at such tales became a celebrity. Much of his work was set to music and printed in sheet form, sales of which were a valuable source of income for him as, for the Victorians, music and rhymes were the principal entertainment of the day. His verses had titles like *How I became a Flute Player* and *The Tragic End of the London Amateur Flute Society*. During his long career as a musician he mixed with most of the leading musical masters and brought many to visit his London home.

The Wells family all became musicians; when Benjamin gave up his place as lead flautist with the Drury Lane Orchestra, he became a popular lecturer of music. He would use his son

Clifford and daughter Elizabeth on pianoforte to accompany the singing of daughters Ada, Kate and Eva as he presented concert lectures on popular music.

Janet was brought up in London in the hubbub of this talented and loving family. She was surrounded by warmth and the family was blessed by the lack of financial concern. Their home was invariably full of music and laughter and one that was also mercifully free of the dangerous killer diseases that took their victims from all strata of society. Indeed, even the Prince of Wales nearly died from the water-borne disease, typhoid. The lurking concern over the ever present dangers from such diseases did not temper the merriment or frivolity of the younger members of the Wells family, guarded, as they were, by their parents' serious regard for the health and welfare of the household. Both the family and their staff happily accepted daily prayers and attendance at church.

Janet, like many little girls, was interested in the daily domestic routine of the household and would spend many happy hours in the kitchen with her mother and the family cook learning how to make cakes and sweets. Two recipes, written out by the ten year-old Janet survive to this day:

Janet Wells' recipes – aged 10 years

Recipe for Toffee

Put into a stewpan 3 lb Raw sugar, a pinch of Cream of Tartar. ¼ lb butter in small pieces.

1 Pint Boiling Water. Stir it about 3 times before it comes to the boil but not after. Should it be likely to boil over put a piece of butter in. When you want to see if it is cooked enough, butter a spoon, take a small quantity out and dip it in cold water, it should at once go hard.

Recipe for Scones

Take 1 lb flour and milk, add to it one and a half teaspoonfuls of baking powder, add a pinch of salt and make into a light dough with ½ pint milk roll out to about ½ an inch in thickness then cut out in rounds and bake in a moderately hot oven for twenty minutes.

Janet and her siblings all attended a nearby private school where Janet excelled at French and other subjects deemed suitable for a 'nice' young English lady of quality. Religion was one of the main subjects taught. Very little emphasis was put on a young girl's academic education as it was considered unladylike for a young lady to pursue a career. If she did, it was automatically assumed that her family was unable to support her. It was a difficult time for young women as wars and migration had unwittingly created a pool of spinsters across the social divide. Social convention discouraged a young woman from competing against the male sex and apart from marriage, there was little left but to assist her mother. The socially accepted future for a young lady of quality was to make a 'good' marriage and bring up her family for God, Queen and Country.

Janet was a bright, pretty girl with a determined character. Her musical talents and ready wit made her a popular member of both her church and school. She had a very strong social conscience and was greatly influenced by the religious and social reformers she heard at meetings regularly held in her church. The stories of Florence Nightingale's exploits in the Crimean War and her part in the campaign and its appalling aftermath held a particular fascination for her and the young, inquisitive teenager absorbed all she could about this remarkable woman.

To her parents, the person who clearly had the greatest influence over the young Janet Wells was Michael Laseron. Dr Michael Maximilian August Heinrich Laseron was a German Jewish immigrant, born in 1819. He qualified as a homeopathic doctor and worked for a while at the Deaconesses' Hospital at Kaiserswerth in Germany, where his experiences caused him to convert to Christianity, much to the dismay of his family and community. Such was the widespread intolerance of his conversion that he was hounded from his position and fled the country.

Arriving in England in the 1850s he set up a pharmacy overlooking the green fields of Tottenham and soon gained a reputation for his good works. He raised funds amongst his fellow churchgoers to open a small refuge for waifs and orphans; he also treated the elderly poor and slum dwellers in their own homes.

Dr Laseron exuded goodness and he attracted a local philanthropist named John Morley, who asked him what project he would most like to see fulfilled. Without a pause, Laseron replied he would like to establish a hospital built on the same lines as Kaiserswerth to train young women not only to be nurses, but also to be devout Christians. He outlined his plans to create a Protestant equivalent to the Catholic Sisters of Mercy, where his nurses could, by their Christian example, spread the word of the Lord.

Mr Morley was impressed enough to fund the project to the tune of £6,000 and the first British Deaconesses' Hospital was opened in London in 1868 (see Appendix B). To enlist suitable recruits, Laseron preached in the chapels of north London on the lines of 'Practical Christianity'. He appealed for 'sisters' and wished:

> ... the ladies who were only ornamental would raise themselves from the indolence of their useless lives and enlist in active, healthy service for Christ.

He promised that the course he recommended would be spiritually uplifting as well as invaluably useful. This promise of saintly virgins quietly and serenely ministering to the grateful sick had a downside. In order to attract only the really dedicated, pay and conditions were pitched low and spartan. Probationer nurses received nothing but their maintenance. When they had been accepted into the order, they were paid seven pounds and seven shillings a year for underclothing and pocket money which, Laseron wrote, 'the sisters found sufficient'. The annual salary of a qualified nursing Superintendent was between £30 and £100.

Not everyone was in full-hearted agreement with this new order. In May 1869, an article appeared in *The Daily Telegraph* which was highly critical of the Protestant Deaconesses' Institution:

While the High Church party in England is making efforts, sometimes vigorous and sometimes weak, to equal the spiritual pretensions and to imitate the histrionic appliances of the Roman Church, the Evangelicals amongst us have curiously turned their thoughts to borrowing from the Church of Rome the practical advantages of one of their charitable organizations. An Evangelical nunnery has been opened at Tottenham.

It is to be called a Deaconesses' Home; but it will be seen, from the rules, that the ladies may be fairly called Protestant nuns. They are to wear white caps and aprons, with dark-coloured dresses and bonnets. They must be addressed as sister. Each sister is to promise to remain at least five years in the service of the institution. Candidates must be over seventeen and under thirty-five years of age. They must not be married, nor have any intention of making such an engagement.

The Tottenham sisters are to be trained nurses; they will have to go into the filthiest lanes and alleys of their district, to nurse persons in infectious diseases, to face pestilence and be ready at all hours to go anywhere and do anything. Then the reasons for a peculiar dress are obvious enough.

There is no doubt that some men exist to insult and annoy ladies simply because they are women; but a Sister dressed in an unbecoming uniform is marked off from ordinary women. In this Protestant country, and amid a population often coarse and rude, there has been no instance, we believe, of a Sister of Mercy being insulted or molested; and we imagine that we owe the protection in a great measure to their distinctive dress . . .

The same view is at the bottom of the prohibition 'engagements'. For a pretty young deaconess to go about her errands, accompanied by her 'young man' would not do; yet if deaconesses during their residence were engaged to be married, who could forbid so natural, yet so distracting, an arrangement? Nor is the denunciation of intentions as absurd as it might seem. It is clearly intended to protect the

43

institution from the mistake of interfering with possible engagements of that kind.

We are, therefore, inclined to believe that the founders of the Tottenham Home are not unwise in shutting out from their precincts all ladies in love.

The report was, however, inaccurate on several counts. It was never intended to be a religious order in the sense in which the term was used for Roman Catholic and Anglican churches. Also the deaconesses were not forbidden to marry but were obliged to consult Dr Laseron if they so intended. Laseron appointed as his first Lady Superintendent a Kaiserswerth-trained sister, Frau Libussa, soon to be replaced by Sister Christian Dundas, who remained in the post for many years.

With the outbreak of the Franco-Prussian War, Laseron volunteered his services to the British Aid Society and, in September 1870, led out a team of four sisters. They were based in Verneville until February 1871 and here they treated mostly sick and wounded Prussians, mainly because of Laseron's German extraction. Sadly, there was an unexpected fatality when one of the sisters contracted dysentery, died, and was buried in Verneville cemetery. The experience confirmed Laseron's belief in the concept of international medical help during periods of conflict wherever wars were fought. In recognition of their efforts, the Empress of Prussia sent a personal letter of thanks and enclosed a Cross of Merit for Women to be deposited with the Institution.

On his return, Laseron became an honorary associate of the Order of St John. He continued to extol his belief in 'Practical Christianity' from the pulpits and stages of London. It was one of these sermons, attended by the seventeen year-old Janet Wells, that delayed her plan to apply to the Nightingale Training School at St Thomas's Hospital in favour of following Dr Laseron.

In 1876 a short but nasty war broke out in the Balkans when the Christian Serbs, bolstered by Russian volunteers, rose up against their Turkish overlords. They were no match for the might of the Ottoman Empire and in just four months the Serbs were soundly defeated. Both sides displayed shocking brutality towards each other in which it became preferable to be killed outright rather than to be left wounded or taken prisoner. Estimates put the number of civilians massacred by the callous irregular Bashi Bazook from the Ottoman Empire as between 15,000 and 30,000 souls.

Dr Laseron and a team of six Deaconess nurses attended both sides during the war and spent three months working in Serbia where Dr Laseron had been severely criticized by the League in Aid of Christians in Turkey, who objected to his even handed treatment of both Turks and Serbs. Conversely, the Serbs accused him of being a Turkish spy; these misunderstandings illustrated the jealousies and tensions that existed between the relief organizations. It was against the background of these events that Janet finally decided to become a nurse and, if called upon, to volunteer for overseas duty. It took a particularly strong minded and dedicated girl to leave the comfort and security of family life. In November 1876, and with the family now living in Islington, Janet's parents gave their support and arranged for her to attend Dr Laseron's Protestant Deaconesses' Training Institute at nearby Tottenham, despite their fears and reservations about her choice of career.

One good thing that emerged from this particular Balkan conflict was the singling out by Vincent Kennet Barrington, who was in charge of transport for the British Aid Society, of Dr Laseron and his nurses for special praise for their effectiveness. He wrote that the departure from St Katherine's Hospital in Belgrade of Dr Laseron and his nurses left a great blank. Although Serbian Sisters replaced them, their absence greatly affected the wounded that they had tended so carefully. Dr Laseron was able to pass on their experiences to his new trainees, who now included the young and very enthusiastic Janet Wells.

Undeterred by what she learned of the hardships she could expect, Janet remained determined to succeed in her chosen vocation. Although she had some experience of charitable visiting in the poorer areas of London, young ladies of her age and class were always steered away from the worst of the slums, so she really had very little knowledge or understanding of the appalling conditions under which the very poor lived. With her enthusiasm for a career in nursing growing by the day, she was soon to find out.

In 1876 Janet Wells was the youngest recruit at just seventeen years of age, but she quickly settled into the trainee nurse regime of the Protestant Deaconesses' Training Institute. The training was based on the same syllabus prescribed by the Nightingale Training School at St Thomas's Hospital with the additional requirement that as an evangelical Christian she was expected to read the gospel daily in the wards, to offer prayers with the patients, and to distribute religious tracts.

Trainees and nurses were required to live in the home attached to the hospital, under the care of a Sister who was responsible for their moral and spiritual character training. The sleeping accommodation was in a large dormitory, very like the wards in the hospital they would work in. A curtain separated each bed and the nurses had a bedside table and a chest in which to keep personal possessions and clothes. A sitting room was provided for the nurses to congregate during their hour off duty. Here the girls were able to relax and pursue their hobbies such as needlework, sketching and reading. The provision of a piano enabled them to enjoy a sing-song together. The girls in the group with Janet were from different backgrounds and had different personalities, and for Janet the idea of communal living was something of an ordeal. Notwithstanding this, all had in common the vocation and dedication to do what is probably the most difficult and heartbreaking, but also the most rewarding, of jobs. The sharing of the traumas and laughter of a long day or night on the wards quickly bonded these girls very closely together, and friendships formed on that first day would last a lifetime.

The probationer nurses were each provided with a uniform and two sets of 'suitable' underwear. When Janet and her fellow trainees entered the dormitory for the first time, each nurse found her new uniform neatly folded on her allocated bed. Being used to fine linen, Janet was amazed to see the heavy cotton drawers, which opened at the crutch. The stockings were equally thick and shapeless. The chemise was cut like a board, being designed to present a shapeless form. Not unnaturally these unsympathetic garments soon underwent a subtle transformation, to which the Home Sister turned a blind eye.

The dresses were made of a pale grey heavy cotton material. They had a long gathered skirt and a fitted bodice cut high at the neck with a detachable white starched collar. The sleeves were long with detachable white starched cuffs. Two white frilled bands were provided so that the sleeves could be rolled up and held in place when necessary to stop the sleeves and cuffs from being soiled during such duties as bed bathing or cleaning. The cap was something of a trial for Janet as the uniform rule prescribed that a nurse's hair should be held off the neck and back off the forehead. The caps caused great merriment to the girls, especially as Janet's hair invariably bobbed down over her forehead – earning her more than one rebuke from Sister. They were bonnets of fine starched cambric, with a small frill round the face and 'strings' (ribbons of matching material), which tied into a neat butterfly bow under the chin. The ribbons were literally a ticklish problem and took some getting used to. Heavily starched pinafore style aprons covered the dresses and as these would be frequently soiled, were changed daily for fresh ones. Pinafores were heavily starched so that when dealing with lousy patients, the lice could not gain a foothold on the smoothly starched fabric. The nurses were grateful for their shiny crisp aprons and were consequently not obliged to hold back from their patients when a medical emergency occurred. Nevertheless, Janet and her colleagues would spend a regular hour with the fine nit comb searching out and removing the eggs or lice from each others' hair.

A long heavy black cloak lined with red flannel and a black uniform dress was also provided for visiting patients in their homes. Treating the poor and the sick at home was very much part of the ethos of the Tottenham Hospital. The work of treating the sick and dying in the slums and mean dens of London went some way to help Janet to cope with the ordeal of her work in the Balkans that was shortly to come.

The hospital superintendent (matron) had undisputed authority over all the trainees. During training Janet and her fellow probationers were to receive practical and theoretical lectures from the senior nursing sisters and the resident medical officer. These lectures included general subjects common to medical and surgical nursing. The duties of the probationer nurse were listed under two headings. Under the first, the nurse was required to be sober, honest, truthful, trustworthy, punctual, quiet and orderly as well as clean and neat. The second required the nurse to be skilful in thirteen separate functions including dressings, the application of leeches, the administration of enemas, the management of trusses and of appliances in uterine complaints, friction to the body and extremities (massage), the management of helpless patients, bandaging, bed-making, attending at operations, 'sick' cookery, ventilation of the ward, cleanliness of utensils, observations of the sick and the management of convalescents.

When Janet went onto her first ward, she was told by the ward sister that she would be shown how her work should be done at least once, or even twice to her satisfaction. She was also told how her work should not be done and why. She was then shown the cupboards where lint, tow, bandages and ointments were kept, and the whereabouts of instruments and utensils; she was shown how to dust, wash and clean the wards, all the equipment and furniture, including the lavatories, the urinals and gratings. She was taught to leave the wheels of the beds facing in one direction and to turn the pillows on the beds so that the openings faced away from the door. These seemed useless and petty rules but were in fact great teachers of discipline and order. To the genteel born Janet this was new territory indeed but yet more was to come.

'The great almighty bedpan!' Janet noted, 'That which dominates the new probationer nurse's life.' She was taught how to place the patient on it, empty it and disinfect it. Like all new probationers, Janet spent many a weary hour, with chapped hands and aching back cleaning and polishing the pans in the cold sluice room. She now learned the universally known truth that for one patient to call for a bedpan immediately triggers the desire in at least six others to empty their bladders, especially at night. The plaintive call 'Nurse, I need a bedpan!' dogged a nurse's every waking hour and even intruded into her dreams.

Janet was shown how to wash helpless patients, especially

men, without exposure, by washing them between blankets. The new young nurses viewed the weekly bed-bath routine with some trepidation. However, being of a phlegmatic nature with a strong sense of the ridiculous, Janet took it all in her stride.

One important aspect of caring for a helpless patient was the prevention of bedsores and Janet was shown how to carefully turn the patient from side to side, massaging the back and other pressure points and watching for the first signs of a sore when changing a draw sheet, bathing a patient, or changing bedding. The debilitated state of many of the undernourished patients particularly predisposed these patients to the risk of bedsores. Once a sore appeared the danger of infection was high and a life threatening situation could quickly develop; any bedsore was immediately reported to the ward sister and the surgeon or physician. Like most nurses, the appearance of a bedsore on one of her patients was considered by Janet as almost a personal insult to her diligence and care.

After only two weeks, Janet and her fellow probationer nurses were taught how to apply dressings, using two basins for washing wounds, and always dipping tow or cotton wool into one basin only; how to make and apply poultices at their proper temperature and also fomentation flannels; how to dress blisters; how to apply iodine and other paints and liniments. They also learned how to give injections and enemata; how to pass catheters on women; how to record a patient's temperature, pulse and respiration; how to make and apply bandages, cover splints and how to use trusses on women.

At first Janet was afraid of causing her patients pain as she carried out these necessary procedures, but she soon learned that a firm, yet gentle, hand moving swiftly but surely caused less pain than trying to dab slowly at an open or infected wound, or dallying around when giving an injection. Although most of her patients were from very different social backgrounds, Janet found it easy to talk to them and would listen to their troubles and worries while she was tending to them.

Every probationer had to learn 'sick' cookery and the use of cooking utensils as well as how to make beef tea and egg flip, when to use beer and wine, and the proportions, and how to make gruel and drinks for the sick. The ward sister taught them how to observe their patients, explaining the reason why medicines were given and why they were altered, as well as the reason for dressings and so on. She also taught them how to describe the different sorts of coated tongues, the differences of sputum and the feeling of pus on skin.

Janet found that assisting in the operating theatre was a fascinating experience but she much preferred to care for conscious patients. The first operation for any young nurse is always a momentous occasion and Janet felt, in common with her fellow probationers, the butterflies in the stomach and the nagging fear of fainting when the first incision was made. The instruction 'if you must faint nurse, do it backwards, away from the operating table' from a mischievous young surgeon did not help either. The surgeon and his assistants operated in their everyday clothes and no masks were worn, while the nurses wore their everyday uniforms, caps and aprons. The operating theatre was an ordinary room, with windows that were usually open on a warm day. A nurse was often stationed at the open window with a fly swat to discourage any flying insects. She was also deputed to wield the carbolic spray, which was used to reduce infection. Large glass instrument cupboards were ranged around the room along with metal and glass trolleys and tables. The operating table stood in the centre of the room with the large operating light over it, a series of mirrors in the bowl of the lamp illuminated the operating table. The electric operating light was an innovation in the hospital operating theatre and made the work of the surgeons considerably easier.

An adjoining room housed the hot water tanks or sterilizers where the instruments were boiled and prepared for the next operation. It was in this room that the large swabs used in operations would be washed and soaked in bleach before being sent to the laundry. A nurse who fumbled when laying up a trolley or made an undue noise could provoke a roar of rage from the surgeon operating. Equally, any noise from the nurses washing the instruments from the previous case in the sluice room on the other side of the operating theatre would provoke a similar reaction.

The probationers also had to learn the necessary precautions to prevent the occupational hazard of finger poisoning through lack of cleanliness when dealing with infected patients. A septic finger for a trainee nurse could lead to generalized septicaemia and death; only the urgent amputation of the finger could save the life of someone infected. The method of preventing the spread of infection, by assiduous hand washing before and after treating every patient, had been discovered twenty-six years earlier by Dr Semmelweiss while working in an obstetric clinic in Vienna. Concerned at the high rate of puerperal fever and a mortality rate of 30 per cent, which colleagues believed was caused by over-crowding, poor ventilation, onset of lactation or 'miasma', he deduced that infection was being carried by medical students from post mortem rooms to healthy mothers in the labour wards. Students were ordered to wash their hands in chlorinated water before each examination and the mortality rate fell to 1.27 per cent. His ideas were not universally accepted even though conventional care continued to cause high mortality rates. He was forced from Vienna and was accepted by the medical profession only when Joseph Lister stated of Semmelweiss 'I think with the greatest admiration of him and his achievement and it fills me with great joy that at last he is given the respect due to him'.

The new nurses were taught to manage convalescent patients especially from typhoid, and the difficult job of preparing a dead body for removal with care and dignity. All this had to be learned whilst spending long arduous hours on the wards. It is hardly surprising that after evening prayers and supper, the probationers took their sore feet and weary bodies to an early bed.

With the bustle and chatter of the day over, night duty proved to be a particularly daunting experience for some of Janet's fellow probationers. After the last bedpan round and the dispensing of milky evening drinks, the night sedations given and the gas lights turned down low, the soft shadows gathered and danced in the flickering night light. Fortunately Janet was not afraid of the dark, nor was she a girl of a nervous disposition. A table and chair drawn close to the comforting warmth of the pot-bellied stove was a small comfort for the night nurse to sit in the quiet reaches of the night to fold swabs and roll bandages for the stock cupboard. However soporific the low shaded light, the counting of the swabs into bundles of ten and the warmth from the stove, Janet remained alert for the slightest sound from one of her patients, and she would walk quietly round the ward at frequent intervals, tucking in a blanket here, rearranging the pillows of a restless patient there, and filling a beaker with water or wiping the face of a fevered patient with a cold flannel. She found night duty a rewarding experience. It was the occasion when she could spend more time with her patients, listening to their problems from home or soothing the pain of someone dying. Her diligence and care did not go unnoticed by her superiors.

All probationer nurses at the Deaconesses' Institution had to attend lectures by the doctors and consultants as well as keeping up their files of case papers and jotting down anything new they had learned during the day. And there was much to learn; during the period when Janet Wells was beginning her career, life in Britain was extremely unhealthy. Malnutrition, tuberculosis, influenza, whooping cough, scarlet fever, measles, and a host of less significant infectious diseases were among the major health problems to which had to be added the pandemic disease of syphilis.

Civilization and syphilization had already gone hand in hand for four centuries, the disease having been imported into Spain by Columbus's sailors following their discovery of Haiti and the sexual delights offered them by the island's generous women. The returning sailors carried the newly acquired syphilitic bacteria *Treponema pallidum* and, as heroes, were fêted by a grateful nation. The bacteria immediately began boring into the bones and skulls of the population and syphilis rapidly spread across Europe to Britain. It had no regard for rank or title; royal houses spread it among their courtesans and the aristocracy while the military rapidly spread it both at home and abroad. There was an almost total acceptance of the effects of the disease with its raging headaches, swollen joints, wart-like lesions and mouthfuls of sores and ulcers. The brain and skeletal structure were frequently affected, as well as the liver, kidney, and other visceral organs. Infection of the heart and major blood vessels accounted for most deaths, often caused by a major rupture of the

52

main blood vessel out of the heart. There was great fear of the disease and some of those who contracted it committed suicide when they were told the diagnosis. The disease continued its unrelenting course until the brain and body were affected by the general paralysis of the insane, destroying both movement and all power of logic.

One particular form of tuberculosis, scrofula, was rife in London and was caused by sufferers spitting contaminated phlegm. This condition eventually gave rise to the familiar 'No spitting' notices which were still common in the 1950s. Across the mainland of Britain, scrofula was especially common amongst children who frequently went barefoot and contracted the disease through the skin of their feet. The only treatments at the time included surgical blood letting, applications of phosphoric acid, ether inhalation and digitalis drinks. Most physicians viewed the disease with professional disinterest until Robert Koch discovered the bacillus in 1882. Diagnosis of the bacterium was still extremely difficult until Paul Ehrlich found that heating the stained slide fixed the coloured dye of the stain to the bacterium and made it much more easily visible.

Janet recalled one macabre experiment involving influenza, which was euphemistically known at the time as 'a jolly rant', 'the new delight', a 'gentle correction' or the 'blue plague'. Her group of trainee nurses was shown how a lung from a healthy body would float in water while that of a flu victim promptly sank. Because it did not disfigure the features, rot the genitals or cripple limbs it was not generally considered to be a serious condition until it developed into pneumonia, especially as influenza rarely killed its victims except in the case of children or the elderly, neither of which warranted social concern at the time. Doctors were not unduly perturbed as the condition created the status quo of medical perfection, of everybody ill and no one dying. The several symptoms of a simple attack would have included a dry cough, sore throat, nasal obstruction and discharge, and burning of the eyes. More complex cases were characterized by chills, sudden onset of fevers, headaches, aching of muscles and joints, and occasional gastrointestinal symptoms. Therefore little medical intervention took place or was considered necessary.

In spite of the hard work, reprimands from senior staff and many tears for a patient lost, especially a child, there was a great deal of laughter and fun. Being an accomplished musician, Janet was a popular member of her nurses' group with her songs and ballads. Many of these were, of course, written by her father. Because the nurses worked long hours and days off were very rare, Janet made frequent diary notes that she missed her family, especially her mother and sisters. They had spent many happy hours together playing their various musical instruments and practising songs. Visits to the park with the younger children to play ball games or bowl-a-hoop were always popular. Janet particularly liked to help sail her brothers' boat on the pond or to fly the kites they had made themselves. She was particularly inventive with paint, paper and string and her kites made a colourful show.

Janet had been training for only ten months when the simmering discontent in the Balkans flared up once again, this time into a full-scale war between Christian Russia and Moslem Turkey. For the fourth time that century the two protagonists had gone to war, ostensibly over religion. This time the focus was on the land east of Serbia, Bulgaria, where there had been a series of nationalist uprisings. These had been brutally put down. As the self-appointed champion of the Slavic peoples and the Orthodox Church, there was great pressure within Russia for the Tsar, Alexander II, to come to the aid of Bulgaria and eject the Turks. The atrocities committed against the Bulgarian population by the ill-disciplined Turkish Bashi-Bazook outraged British public opinion, which generally sided with the Russians and Bulgarians. Public figures like Charles Darwin, Anthony Trollope, William Morris and Thomas Carlyle put their weight behind the Bulgarian cause and rallies and meetings were held pledging support.

On the other hand, with the Crimean War still fresh in everyone's memory, the military were supportive of the Turks. Several British officers offered their services to the Turkish cause, including Charles Hobart, an ex-Royal Navy Captain, who was appointed Commander of the Black Sea Fleet. Valentine Baker, a former colonel of the 10 Hussars, served as Pasha in charge of the gendarmerie. Colonel Frederick Burnaby, reputed to be the tallest and strongest man in the British Army, managed to get himself appointed to the Stafford House Committee, whose role was organizing volunteer nurses for foreign wars. He used his appointment not to bring relief to the wounded, but to help Baker outmanoeuvre the numerically superior Russian forces at the Battle of Tashkessan to allow the Turks to escape.

The Disraeli government, while not approving of the Turkish action, nevertheless supported the Ottoman Empire as a bulwark against Russian expansion into the Mediterranean via the Balkans and Bosporus. It was not out of the question that Britain would send forces to support Turkey if it appeared that the Russians would gain these strategic goals. The Liberals, under William Gladstone, saw things differently and supported the Bulgarians in their quest for independence. Although Britain was loath to involve herself in European conflicts, as demonstrated during the recent Franco-Prussian War, she was prepared to send volunteer doctors and nurses under the umbrella of the newly formed International Red Cross organization.

With the outbreak of the Russo-Turkish War, there were calls for volunteers to go and tend the wounded in this far-off region. The British Aid Society sent medical help and supplies to both sides. In Turkey, they worked in conjunction with the poorly organized Turkish version of the Red Cross. The Turks had been signatories of the Geneva Convention but found the symbol of the Red Cross repugnant, with its connotations of the hated Crusades, and so were granted a far more acceptable title, the Red Crescent, and duly adopted the motif as its symbol. The Stafford House Committee for the Relief of Sick and Wounded Soldiers sent teams of doctors and ambulances to aid the Turks.

The British Aid Society again approached the Protestant Deaconesses for volunteer nurses. Although she had only been training for a short time, Janet had shown such promise that despite her youth and inexperience, she was chosen by Dr Laseron to be one of a party of nine nurses to go and help the Russian Red Cross in Bulgaria. Janet's British passport, which comprised a single sheet with two elaborate coats of arms and the double-headed eagle visa stamp of Tsarist Russia, was issued.

Meanwhile, with the British medical party approaching the front line, the Russians stubbornly declined British help and requested only financial aid. As this was against the spirit of the Red Cross, Britain refused. As the casualty list quickly grew, so the Russians relented and allowed in the advance party of volunteers with their supplies. The first party of surgeons with three wagonloads of supplies arrived in Bucharest on 22 September 1877. At first the British party was confined to treating the sick and wounded in the Bucharest hospitals but as the casualty lists increased they were needed nearer to the fighting.

Chapter Six

Off to war, putting theory into practice . . .

Sister Janet, as she was now called, bade her apprehensive family farewell and joined eight of her fellow nurses to catch the train to Dover. This was the first time the eighteen year-old had been on a boat of any kind and the excitement of the cross-Channel voyage distracted her thoughts from the gruelling and dangerous trip across Europe that lay ahead of her. The English Channel was quite rough but Janet proved to be an excellent sailor and enveloped in the long warm cloak, which was part of her uniform, she thoroughly enjoyed the fresh air and the sight of the white-capped waves.

On arrival at Calais, the party of volunteers boarded the train that would carry them on the first leg of the arduous five-day journey across the Continent, travelling through Munich, Vienna and Budapest to the Romanian capital of Bucharest. The train was cold as there was no heating, but the girls were given foot warmers, which were slim metal containers filled with hot water that were available from platform staff for a small charge. When wrapped in a blanket this object kept their feet warm and they were refilled at each main stop. Once they entered Romania, their train was frequently delayed to make way for troop trains.

Three days later they reached Bucharest and were received by the local Red Cross Commissioner, Mr Kirkman Loyd, who had made the Hotel de Boulevard the Society Headquarters. Here the weary nurses were able to refresh themselves with hot baths and some very welcome properly cooked food. Janet and her companions already realized from their experience of obtaining accommodation and meals across southern Europe that they had to put their linguistic abilities into full practice; the only languages even partially understood were French or German, English being almost unknown.

Having been briefed on the situation at the front, which was dire, the nurses had their passports endorsed by the Russian military and were soon on their way to the scattered field hospitals that had sprung up on the Danubian Plain. They followed the main route south to the front. First they caught the train to the village of Fratesti, a Red Cross depot, just five miles short of the Danube which was the southern border with Bulgaria. Here the Russians had built a shelter for about 6,000 wounded, where they could rest before being shipped back to Bucharest. There were no beds, so the men lay on filthy soiled straw on the cold mud floor. The chances of survival for these seriously wounded men were very low. If their injuries did not kill them, sickness from the appalling conditions was more than likely to cause their death. Although the train continued on to the town of Giugevo, it was within range of the guns from the Turkish fortress on the opposite bank at Tustchuk, and so Fratesti was chosen as the main terminus.

From Fratesti their mode of transport consisted of nothing more than rough wooden open peasant carts on which they had to endure a journey of some sixty miles westwards, following the course of the Danube. This famous river, celebrated in music and song was certainly not a romantic blue to Janet and her companions. The muddy rutted track had frozen solid from weeks of frost-hardened north-easterly wind blowing across the Moldavian plain from Siberia. The nurses were heading for the principal Russian crossing point at Semnitza, where the Red Cross had set up their advanced stores depot. What they found was a wretched little place, where mud had been churned into foot-deep slime. One nurse noted that the village was '. . . the most miserable place, principally populated as far as I can see, by pigs'. This bleak scene was made worse by the unfriendly and suspicious attitude of the Russians, who viewed all foreigners as spies. For a while, the volunteer British surgeons were barred from crossing into Bulgaria and were only allowed to attend the wounded on the Romanian side of the border. The nurses, however, were allowed to proceed on their journey.

Sister Janet and her colleagues had been ordered to go to Vardin, which was a further forty miles along the Bulgarian riverbank. The bridges at Vardin, where the river was over 300 yards across, had been destroyed so they crossed the impressive bridge of boats, which the Russians had built after the fall of Sistova, and found that they had to wait for an escort for the final part of their journey.

Sistova was overcrowded with fleeing civilian refugees mixing with apprehensive soldiers. It was chaotic and to make things worse, an outbreak of typhus had recently swept through the town. With over 6,000 sick and wounded to care for, mostly from Plevna, the nurses were soon hard at work.

Besides the typhus outbreak and numerous casualties with untreated wounds, there were outbreaks of a variety of other diseases associated with Victorian warfare. Dysentery, bronchitis, diarrhoea and rheumatism were all made worse by a local form of malaria, Danubian fever. The nurses found that with the limited supplies they were carrying, the best they could do was to try and bring some comfort to the many hundreds of wounded and dying soldiers allocated to each of them. Blankets and mattresses were at a premium and could only be given to the severest cases. The nurses cleaned and dressed the many reeking wounds and limb stumps with carbolic solution and the Lister antiseptic dressings. They fed patients with soups, lime juice, cocoa, preserved vegetables and a popular beverage called Liebling's Extract of Meat. They hoped that improving the nutrition of these sick men would enable them to fight the infection and fever which rampaged through the town.

Since the third abortive attempt by the Russians to take Plevna, over 120,000 Russians and Romanians had besieged Osman Pasha's Turkish army with 522 artillery pieces. With food running low and the constant bombardment causing numerous casualties, the Turks attempted to fight their way out. On 10 December they managed to overrun the Russian frontline but were so outnumbered that Osman Pasha, who had been wounded, was forced to surrender. For days on end, the ragged, shuffling line of prisoners passed through Sistova and across the long bridge of boats. Sometimes prisoners were shot simply on the whim of the Russian guards, a terrifying scene that Sister Janet was to repeatedly witness during the next few months. Tens of thousands had been killed on both sides and a similar number were left to die. The stench of death was so severe that the English nurses had to tie camphor-soaked handkerchiefs round their faces to deaden the smell of corruption. Turkish and Bulgarian civilians, especially women and children, had been barbarically treated by the retreating Russians who lay waste towns and villages through which they passed; it was their revenge for the earlier treatment of Russian civilians at the hands of the Turkish troops. Abuse by the Turks of local women had been widespread and a report in the *Daily News*, dated 1 November 1876 reads:

> Thousand have lately fled from the scene of the Turkish massacres; the little ones whose parents have been murdered; mothers whose children have been torn from their arms to suffer a frightful death; young girls on whom has been inflicted the utmost torture and disgrace. These outraged and now homeless and starving creatures cry to us for help . . .

Over 43,000 Turkish troops passed into Russian captivity, which was a death sentence for most of them. Thousands perished in the snows of mid-winter as they were marched at bayonet point into captivity in Russia, their way marked by the thousands of frozen bodies left by the roadside. The English nurses were horrified to see local people and refugees scurrying around among the dead and dying, foraging for anything of value or that might be useful. It was gently pointed out to the nurses that these people, the survivors of appalling atrocities, had nothing themselves and any surviving members of their families were starving.

Thirty years later, a ship docked at Bristol carrying thirty tons of human bones from Plevna; the cargo was ground and used as bone meal to enrich England's parks and gardens.

For Sister Janet, the genteel teenager, it was an awesome baptism of fire, dealing not only with terrible wounds and diseases, but also fearsome looking men with whom she could not communicate. Taking strength in the fellowship of her companions, and in her strong religious belief that God was guiding her, she knew she would come through the ordeal.

At last, transport and an escort were provided and the nurses set off to the east to join the Russian army under the command of the Tsarevitch, now fighting along the River Lom. The snow lay deeply and the endless flat countryside offered few landmarks. The only civilians they saw were traumatized and unseeing. A doctor, Armand Leslie, wrote home:

No pen could ever attempt a description of the scenes and atrocities witnessed here. They simply beggar description... Large numbers die of hunger and thirst. The women are frequently demented, and all are completely paralysed by shock. Their looks are haggard, their minds blank.

As darkness fell it became clear that the party of nurses was totally lost and with no houses or buildings in sight, there was no shelter to be found. The sisters were forced to spend the night in the open carts, huddled together for warmth, their sheepskins frozen by the icy cold. The freezing temperature and the howling of prowling wolves nearby prevented any possibility of sleep. Tired and hungry, the nurses finally reached their destination of Vardin, a village behind the Russian lines on the River Lom and their 'home' for the next few months.

This was not the sort of field hospital that any of the nurses had experienced before. Instead of being concentrated in one particular area, Vardin sprawled into the bleak surrounding snow-covered hills. There was no accommodation available so, while tents were sought, the nurses had to resort to sleeping in the freshly dug graves, covered only with branches and brambles. This offered scant protection from the bitter cold of the Bulgarian mid-winter or the dangers from foraging wild animals. Eventually, the nurses were given a rough wooden hut with planks for beds but sanitation was non-existent. At least the girls were able to change their underwear for the first time since they left Sistova and to help each other with brushes and nit combs to remove the lice and nits from their hair.

As soon as they had unloaded their kit and supplies, they were put to work by the sorely pressed Russian medical staff. Janet estimated that she was allocated about 200 seriously wounded patients who lay in mud hovels scattered in various locations among the hills. Carrying a meagre pack of essential medical supplies, Janet daily trudged through the snow, going from hut to hut, and dealing with the most appalling medical emergencies. She was invariably unescorted.

Each nurse carried her own supply of instruments, essential for treating the worst wounds. Janet often had to work by the light of a small candle, the brass and paper lanterns used in the hospitals being too heavy for her to carry. Where possible, she made a small fire to melt the snow to make a solution of carbolic to clean the filthy wounds. Some were already gangrenous. She frequently had to cut off the putrid, blood soaked dressings and slice away dead gangrenous tissue. She dressed the wounds, regretting the scarcity of the Lister dressings. At least the bandages were clean. She cleansed the men who were suffering from dysentery and diarrhoea. There was little she could do to ease the cause of their pain or give them the sort of food they needed to resist the disease. She had to close her eyes and ears to the death and the suffering that now filled her days.

Taking the advice of a Russian doctor, Janet acquired a long Cossack knife, called a *kinjal*, and a cudgel for self-protection as she made her rounds. These were not only for use against any marauding bandit with rape on his mind but also to fight off the packs of starving dogs and wolves that terrorized the area. Wild and rabid animals frequently attacked the unprotected and helpless wounded and Janet soon got used to scaring them off. On one occasion she was making her way through the woods to her next call, when she was confronted by such a pack of dogs. They managed to knock her to the ground but she was able to keep them at bay with her dagger and club until her cries were heard and the dogs were chased off. The event was well publicized by the *Illustrated Naval & Military Magazine* in March 1885:

More than once these brutes, their mouths reeking with human blood, had her down, but her stick and dagger protected her until her cries brought assistance.

Wild dogs were not the only creatures to terrorize the sisters; ferocious rats infested the whole area and added to the overall misery the nurses had to endure.

Provisions became so scarce at Vardin that the sisters obtained permission to travel to Sistova to procure basic rations. Here they found that conditions had worsened. Another outbreak of typhus had gripped the town. There was little food to be had, and the essential supplies of carbolic and bandages were running low. Janet managed to find a small bottle of tincture of laudanum, which would ease the pain of the most seriously injured. On returning to Vardin, they were told that their movements were now restricted and the nurses were effectively treated like prisoners. Despite this unfriendly attitude, Sister Janet and her companions continued to do what they could for the wretched wounded. During a period when the Russians believed that the British would actively side with the Turks, they ungallantly cut off all fresh rations to the British nurses. The sisters were forced to live on two week-old slabs of coarse black bread, rock-hard from age and freezing temperatures. At night, they would use the bread as pillows and cover their faces to deter the rats that would come and gnaw at the bread while they slept.

One night, the cover fell off the face of one of the sisters, and she was badly bitten about her mouth and chin. Janet and her friends nursed her carefully and tenderly, fearing that the wounds would become septic, or worse, infect her with one of the horrific diseases known to be carried by vermin. Supplies of Eusol and Gentian Violet had run out and the carbolic would have done too much damage. Fortunately one of the Russian doctors volunteered the last few drops of brandy in his flask to dab on her wounds as an antiseptic. Thankfully their administrations were successful and, although scarred, she made a speedy recovery.

Not all of Sister Janet's patients were Russian soldiers. In rare examples of mercy, several wounded Bashi-Bazook had been spared torture and death and had been taken prisoner. On two separate occasions, these unpredictable brigand prisoners had attacked Janet. One prisoner had attempted to stab her while the other had tried to bludgeon her as she leaned over to dress his wounds. Whether out of fear, blood lust or delirium, no one bothered to ask, for on each occasion the miscreant was immediately dragged outside and shot.

Despite the dedication and care lavished on the wounded by the sisters, the attitude of the Russians remained distinctly hostile and unceasingly suspicious. Supplies and communication across the Danube stopped. Letters to and from home went undelivered and the Russians made it clear to the nurses that all British volunteers were still regarded as prisoners, but that they should continue their duties. Sister Janet and her companions later learned that the British Government, alarmed at Russian successes, had threatened war if Russia occupied all of Turkey including Constantinople. The British Army was mobilized to the extent that some Indian units were sent to Malta to prepare to intervene. In the end, a Royal Navy squadron was dispatched to the Bosporus, which was enough to deter the Russians from occupying the city. For a while, war between Britain and Russia was a distinct possibility and, until diplomacy prevailed, it was the British Aid Society volunteers who bore the brunt of Russian anger.

After about three months enduring the privations of Vardin, the sisters were ordered to travel to the Shipka Pass, which had seen some of the most ferocious fighting of the war. The pass rose to an altitude of 5,000 feet and followed a tortuous path along a ridgeline for ten miles. In several desperate encounters, the Russians just managed to retain control. In one last-ditch stand, the Russian defenders ran out of ammunition and resorted to hurling rocks down on the Turks. The toll in lives was high; 3,640 Russians and over 10,000 Turks were killed. Turkish resistance was beginning to crack. The Tsarevitch's army had beaten Suleiman Pasha on the Lom and pushed him back to the Danube town of Rustchuk to the north; the British nurses were ordered to follow. Months of living on a starvation diet had left them emaciated and weak; most had contracted typhus and were in no condition to travel. Sister Janet, despite her own weakened state, made her sick companions as comfortable as possible by laying them on mattresses in the carts and making frequent stops. After a long and gruelling journey through the devastated country littered with rotting carcasses of humans and animals, where the sky seemed permanently filled with the black shapes of circling carrion crows, they reached the Tsarevitch's army before Rustchuk.

Sister Janet was now obliged to spend most of her time nursing her companions. Relief came in the nick of time as the Turks capitulated and the war was virtually over. The Russian attitude changed with victory and, in a complete about-turn, praise was heaped on the nurses. Janet met the Tsarevitch, who learned of her dedicated work among the Russian wounded and insisted that she should sleep in his quarters until she was ready to make the journey back to Bucharest. Back in the capital, she reported to the Commissioner at the Hotel de Boulevard, who took her to dine with their star prisoner, the Turkish hero of Plevna, Osman Pasha.

Although individual male colleagues acknowledged the work that Sister Janet and her companions had performed, the official British line was one of embarrassed deafening silence. In spite of all the work that Florence Nightingale had done together with the British Aid Society, it seemed that nurses were still underestimated and viewed by the authorities as little more than servants. After recovering her strength, Janet made the long journey back to London. The train journey seemed almost luxurious after the privations of the previous months.

Janet and her companions had all survived; it was an experience that would have tried the most hardened and experienced of military men. It was only much later that Janet and her party were recognized for their contribution to the war when the Russian government awarded each member of this small but exceptionally brave band of British nurses the Imperial Order of the Red Cross of Russia.

Meanwhile, Britain went to war in South Africa against the Zulus.

CHAPTER SEVEN

The Anglo Zulu War

All without the permission of the British government . . .

T he Wells family were overjoyed and very relieved to see their daughter safely returned home though they were shocked at her emaciated appearance and her weakened state of health. Following the well-reported Balkan war via the newspapers, many events during the war had caused them a great deal of anxiety and they had feared for her safety, especially when the Russians had declared the British party prisoners and had cut off all outside communication to the nurses. Janet now needed time to rest and recuperate at the family's Islington home in north London. The appalling diet and deprivation of nutrition over the recent months had caused her teeth to loosen and her thick curly hair to become thin and wispy. Often at night she would dream she was back at Vardin and would wake herself shouting at the imaginary wild dogs and frantically seeking her *kinjal* to fight them off. At first she was happy just to be pampered but, as her health improved and she regained her strength, the nightmares receded and her thoughts turned to her future. She knew that she wanted more than anything else to continue with her nursing career, and, if required, would be prepared to enter the field of conflict again.

When only two weeks into her well-earned recuperation, Janet's parents were shocked by their daughter's announcement that she intended to return to the Laseron Hospital in Tottenham and understandably tried to dissuade her. Her quiet determination, however, persuaded them that this was her true vocation and they recognized that their merry, pretty young daughter had become a much graver, mature young woman. After only three weeks' leave it was with some sadness that they accompanied her to the Laseron Hospital in Tottenham along with large supplies of restorative invalid delicacies such as calves-foot jelly and cod liver oil of malt.

Meanwhile, the Protestant Deaconesses had built up a reputation to rival those of the St Thomas's trained nurses and were now called on to send their nurses all over the country to newly opened hospitals desperate for experienced nurses to supervise their own untrained staff. In the case of the Sunderland Infirmary, where eight Laseron trained nurses had been sent, the hospital had its complement increased first to twelve nurses and eventually to eighteen and became a nurses' training centre in its own right. In a rare show of praise for a rival training hospital, Florence Nightingale responded to an urgent request for a trained nurse from a hospital in Buckingham.

> I am afraid it is no use – I think very highly of Dr Laseron's place now, but they also have not one to spare. They supply Aberdeen, Perth and elsewhere with hospital nurses.

The Tottenham Hospital authorities considered that Janet was now experienced and capable enough to hold a position of responsibility so that, on receiving a request from Newcastle-upon-Tyne, she was sent to the north-east of England as Nursing Superintendent at the Newcastle Hospital, a remarkable position for the nineteen year-old. This appointment was a very important part of Janet's training. It was here that she had the opportunity to exercise her organizational skills, teaching ability and the diplomatic art of persuading a disparate group of people to work together in harmony, a very necessary skill to ensure the smooth running of a large general hospital. It was however, an assignment that lasted but a few months.

During the early part of 1879 and while Sister Janet was resting at her parents' home in London, two fresh conflicts broke out involving the British Army. In Afghanistan, another war had begun with the spectre of Russia moving vast numbers of troops ever closer to Imperial India. Thwarted by Britain at the Berlin Congress, which robbed her of her triumph over the Turks, Russia massed 15,000 troops on the Afghanistan border and provocatively sent a mission to Kabul. Britain's response was to insist on the Afghans accepting a British mission; they refused. Stung by the Afghan rejection, a large Anglo-Indian force was assembled on the North-West Frontier of India and war was declared. This dispute held the promise of a long and bitter conflict and its seriousness was reflected in the numbers of reporters who were dispatched to cover the looming war. In the event it was to be a totally unexpected conflict that would grasp the public's attention.

In southern Africa, a much smaller affair was stuttering along and was thought to be of such little significance that only one newspaper bothered to send a correspondent. During 1877–8, two local tribes, the Gallika and Gaika, had caused serious problems for British settlers by constantly raiding their cattle in the sparsely populated area of Kaffararia, which lay between the British Cape Colony and Natal. At the request of Sir Bartle Frere, the High Commissioner for South Africa, additional troops were sent to bolster the protracted and weakly conducted campaign and a new, more determined, Army commander was appointed, Lieutenant General Frederick Thesiger, soon to be elevated to Lord Chelmsford on the death of his father. Both Frere and the new commander were old friends from their respective services in India and Frere quickly convinced Chelmsford of his vision for uniting southern Africa. Frere believed that the absorption of small independent African states would bring strength and stability to the area and harmoniously bring the whole region of southern Africa under the rule of the British Crown, as had been successfully achieved in India and Canada.

By the mid-summer of 1878, Chelmsford had subdued the belligerent tribes in what became known as the Ninth Frontier War. Plans to invade Zululand were immediately drawn up, despite the fact that the Zulu monarch, King Cetshwayo, was well disposed towards the British in Natal and did not seek military confrontation. Having built up a considerable force of Imperial troops and colonial volunteers, Frere deliberately provoked a war by issuing an ultimatum demanding the disbanding of the Zulu army, which was correctly calculated to be unacceptable to the Zulu king. Despite conciliatory messages from King Cetshwayo, Lord Chelmsford's force began their unopposed invasion of Zululand on 11 January 1879 when they crossed the border at three points, and all without the knowledge or permission of the British government. The Centre Column consisted of the two battalions of the 24 (2nd Warwickshire) Regiment, together with six guns of the Royal Artillery, mounted Colonial volunteers and 600 poorly led dissident Zulus who made up the Natal Native Contingent. All confidently crossed the Buffalo River at the isolated site of the mission station of Rorke's Drift. A few days later an easily won skirmish against a weak Zulu force at Sihayo's homestead reinforced Chelmsford's conviction that if he could bring the Zulu army to battle, he would emerge victorious.

After ten days, the long unwieldy column had travelled only twelve miles through swampy gorges that seriously hampered their progress. Finally they emerged into a wide valley dominated by an impressive looking rock formation called Isandlwana. Here the British invasion force rested and established a substantial camp. Supplies were brought up from their main depot at nearby Rorke's Drift and as the troops erected their tents and cooking fires, scouting parties were dispatched to look for the approaching Zulu army.

One of these reconnaissance patrols was sent off in the direction of the Zulu capital at Ulundi and after some fifteen miles observed several hundred advancing Zulus; the patrol immediately reported the Zulu presence back to Chelmsford as darkness fell. In his eagerness to confront the enemy, Chelmsford convinced himself that the main Zulu army lay in that direction and so he decided to take half his force and, through the night, marched east, leaving all his equipment, supplies and the balance of his command in camp. Certain that the camp would be dismantled and moved forward to join him during the following twelve hours, little provision was made to defend the camp. The next day, 22 January, was stifling hot; Chelmsford and his men reached the point where the Zulus had been seen during the previous evening and then spent a frustrating morning chasing groups of Zulu warriors who would appear on the surrounding hilltops and, before they could be engaged, melted away into the surrounding valleys. During this time, he received a number of messages from the camp, which became increasingly alarming as the day wore on. The final message was barely credible as it reported that thousands of Zulus were swiftly advancing on the camp. Indeed, this was so.

The luckless Lieutenant Colonel Pulleine, who had never seen any military action, had been left in charge of the movement of the Isandlwana camp and his orders were simple: to break camp and then follow Chelmsford. When the Zulus first appeared on the hills overlooking his Isandlwana camp, Pulleine had thrown out a wide skirmish line of soldiers along the front of the position, supported by the two 7-pounder guns of the Royal Artillery. Although Zulus were massing on the hills, no undue alarm was felt and Pulleine ordered half his command to continue to dismantle the camp. Unbeknown to the hapless colonel, the 25,000 strong Zulu army had hidden only five miles away behind the line of hills to the north of the camp. Their diversionary ploy of splitting Chelmsford's command by drawing him east had worked to perfection. Now the Zulu army prepared to attack the unsuspecting, outnumbered and near-defenceless camp. Meanwhile, completely unseen by the British, the attacking Zulu right wing had been sent to work their way around the un-defended side of Isandlwana, using the ridge of the mountain as a screen. In an impressive example of control, the Zulus managed to bring all their warriors into battle in their classic enveloping 'horns of the buffalo' movement. In one brilliantly coordinated attack, the tented area of the camp was then overrun from behind by the Zulu right wing, which had appeared from the un-defended side of the mountain, while the Zulu centre and left horn pushed into the thinly spread line of defending redcoats. With their camp overrun from behind, the British soldiers were surrounded and any thought of retreat was now impossible. Hacked down in increasing numbers, small groups of them made doomed last-ditch stands until overwhelmed.

In a very short time it was all over and the British suffered their greatest defeat to a native army, losing nearly 1,400 men. Only a few survivors managed to escape before the camp was completely surrounded. The survivors then had to endure a terrifying ride across a trackless route strewn with boulders and bisected by deep gullies, harried all the way by fleet-of-foot Zulu warriors until they reached the Buffalo River. Here they found the mighty river in full spate from the recent heavy rains but, with no alternative route, the survivors were forced to plunge into the 150-yards wide raging torrent. Many drowned or were killed on the bank by Zulu gunfire, but those eighty or so who managed to cross the river headed as fast as they could for the nearest military refuges at Helpmekaar and Rorke's Drift.

Those few survivors who passed by the store and hospital at Rorke's Drift brought news to the small garrison of the unbelievable disaster at Isandlwana and warned the incredulous soldiers there of the Zulu approach. Unable to retreat to Helpmekaar because of the sick and wounded in the hospital, it was decided that B Company of the 2/24 Regiment, who had been detached to guard Chelmsford's supplies and hospital, should remain to defend the converted mission building. There were plenty of sacks and boxes with which to build a good fortification and soon ramparts of biscuit boxes and mealy sacks were erected. The last minute desertion by the 200 or so Natal Native Contingent meant that the garrison was reduced to 139, of whom only 104 were fit to fight. A combination of good organization, superior firepower and great bravery was enough to hold 4,000 Zulus at bay for twelve hours. The heroic defence of Rorke's Drift was lavishly rewarded with eleven Victoria Crosses, including the greatest number ever awarded to a regiment for a single battle. The action was hailed as a great feat of arms but it could not lessen the scale of the disaster that had befallen the British Army at Isandlwana.

Lord Chelmsford led his traumatized command back across the Buffalo River and into the safety of Natal, where, following the defeat at Isandlwana, the white population waited in great trepidation for the feared Zulu invasion of their farms and towns. In the event there would be no Zulu invasion, but hastily prepared forts were nevertheless constructed. At nearby Helpmekaar and at the ruins of the Rorke's Drift mission, where the Zulus had set fire to the hospital during the battle, all medical supplies had been destroyed. All that the doctors could muster were those medicines they carried in their saddlebags. Very soon the unsanitary conditions, made worse by the cold drenching rains and the almost total absence of medical care, caused great suffering among the demoralized soldiers. Typhoid broke out and the victims had to be isolated in thin leaky tents erected outside the military camps. Nobody could escape the scourge of dysentery, rheumatism and camp fever that swept through the crowded and unsanitary camps, and the doctors and senior officers were powerless to alleviate their men's suffering.

One major problem was the slow line of communication with Britain. At that time, the telegraph from Britain terminated at Madeira so messages had to be carried the remainder of the way by ship. News of the Isandlwana disaster took over three weeks to reach Britain, so the response to urgent calls for medical supplies and personnel would take at least two months to reach South Africa. By contrast, the telegraph already linked Britain with India and with Bucharest during the Russo-Turkish War so news and demands for medical assistance could be quickly acted upon. It would be several months before the telegraph cable was extended to Cape Town.

Meanwhile, the small and overextended Army Medical Department did its best. Makeshift hospitals were set up at such border villages as Ladysmith, the nearest settlement to Helpmekaar and Rorke's Drift, and Utrecht and Newcastle in the north. Without adequate supplies and medicines, the sick list grew and deaths mounted.

These were the days of pre-censorship and soldiers freely wrote home, graphically describing their miserable conditions. With public attention now suddenly switched from events in Afghanistan to Zululand, there were numerous reports of disturbing events and many of the soldiers' letters were published in British and Natal daily newspapers and weekly journals. Archibald Forbes of the *Daily News* was especially scathing in his criticism of Lord Chelmsford. It became very clear to the British government and newspaper readers that the High Command in South Africa, in the shape of the defeated Lord

Chelmsford, was now paralysed and unable to inspire their Army. Whatever the mitigating circumstances, and there may have been a few, Chelmsford was regarded as 'an unlucky commander'.

A week after the news of the defeat at Isandlwana had been received by a stunned Whitehall, General Sir Garnet Wolseley learned that the Foreign Office was actively considering replacing Chelmsford as the commander in South Africa. 'Our Only General', as the press dubbed Wolseley, was not greatly enjoying his appointment administrating the British occupation of Cyprus, acquired in the aftermath of the Russo-Turkish War, and he was anxious to get back into an active command. On hearing of the plans to replace Chelmsford, Wolseley, who was definitely a 'lucky commander', immediately put his name forward. It was to take another twelve weeks before his appointment was confirmed, not only as Chelmsford's replacement, but also as Governor of Natal and the Transvaal, as well as the strangely titled 'High Commissioner for Native and Foreign Affairs to the Northward and Eastward of those Colonies'. This was a devious means of sidelining Sir Bartle Frere, who was still greatly respected by Queen Victoria. Not famed for his modesty, Wolseley wrote:

Nothing could be more unpromising or more fraught with danger than the existing condition. Of course a happy stroke of fortune might end the war at any moment, but I confess to see no probability of it under present circumstances, with a demoralized army, the men of which, in all ranks, are thoroughly sick of the war, and have lost all confidence apparently with their leaders. It is very probable that I shall find myself forced to postpone all operations till January, which would create a bad impression at home politically speaking, and would be a fearful disappointment to the Ministry; however, they have only themselves to blame for not having sent me here three months ago.

Wolseley's methods, ideas and energy flew in the face of the military establishment as personified by the reactionary

Commander-in-Chief, the Duke of Cambridge. One of the subjects that concerned Wolseley was the well being and health of his men and he was shocked at the numbers of men unable to perform their duties because of sickness. Major General R.E. Barnsley of the Army Medical Department wrote of this period:

> Our great commanders had never learned that disease has always been more destructive than the most devastating engines of war which the mind of man conceived. None realized that the preservation of the troops was the final responsibility not of medical officers but of commanding officers.

Even Wolseley had earlier commented negatively on field medical officers in his outspoken manual, *The Soldier's Pocket Book*:

> So long as this fad continues, my recommended action is to leave him at the base where he may find some useful occupation as a member of the Sanitary Board.

Unlike most of his contemporaries, however, Wolseley was now prepared to change his mind and accept medical help from outside the military establishment and for this his wife, Lady Louise, must be acknowledged.

CHAPTER EIGHT

No effort had been made . . .

to afford aid from England to our sick and wounded soldiers.

George Granville Leveson-Gower, the grandly titled Duke of Sutherland (1815–91) was a statesman of considerable stature. He had been Foreign Secretary on three occasions, President of the Council, leader of the House of Lords and Colonial Secretary. He also had a philanthropic nature and was an early patron of the International Red Cross. The British Aid Society had been slow in deciding whether or not to become involved in the Serb-Turkish War of 1876, so the Turkophile Duke decided to form a charitable fund for the relief of Turkish sick and wounded. In December that year, he gathered together an impressive array of leading politicians and peers, soldiers and sailors as well as men already involved with other charitable organizations. The eminent war correspondent William Howard Russell was also in attendance. The once-notorious scourge of the establishment, Russell had succumbed to the glitter of high society and become a confidant of the Prince of Wales, even acting as his private secretary during Edward's tour of India in 1874. This all-male roll call of the great and the good met at the Duke's London home called Stafford House, in St James's, and formed themselves into a committee named after the venue.

They never intended to be a rival to the Red Cross but acted in conjunction with them. With so many influential members, funds were readily raised and volunteers were plentiful. When the

Russo-Turkish War began in 1877, they were able to respond without delay and quickly sent volunteers, medicines and an ambulance to help the ramshackle Turkish medical service. One of their volunteers, a Mr Vachall, had been wounded and captured by the Russians who nursed him back to health and returned him to England. Although the sheer numbers of sick and wounded overwhelmed all those who had gone to help, the committee, nevertheless, could feel that they had contributed to improving the conditions for many of the unfortunate victims of the war, both military and civilian.

As was so often the case with such influential people, the aims of Sutherland's committee were not altogether altruistic. There was an element of seeking something more tangible than gratitude at the end of the war. In the case of the Russo-Turkish conflict, Sutherland sought approval from the Sultan to build a railway, to be named the Euphrates Valley Railway, which would link Constantinople with the Persian Gulf. Later, it was hoped, another line could be built through to India. The idea came to nought as the British government refused to support the scheme and it was initially left to the French, and later the Germans, to take up the challenge.

The Stafford House Committee also involved itself with other commercial schemes such as the Anglo-Belgian plan to exploit the potential of the Upper Congo, a trading concession in Zanzibar and, intriguingly, a privately funded plan to save General Gordon at Khartoum. None of these schemes advanced beyond the initial committee stage but the members still met as a 'think tank'.

When news of the British defeat at Isandlwana and the plight of the sick and wounded soldiers reached the Duke of Sutherland, he reconvened the committee. The British Aid Society had decided not to send volunteers but to supply, instead, 'comforts' to the hospitals in Natal. The Stafford House Committee felt that there was plenty of scope for professional assistance rather than just sending socks, newspapers and tobacco. They dropped their all-male configuration and admitted Baroness Angela Burdett-Coutts, one of the wealthiest and most influential women of the age. She was the heiress to the Coutts Bank fortune and used her wealth in such worthy causes as establishing a shelter for 'fallen' women and building model homes. In 1881, at the age of sixty-seven, she scandalized English society by marrying a man thirty-seven years her junior. Even a personal appeal from Queen Victoria could not prevent the union which, despite its potentially unpromising prospects, evolved into a solid and contented marriage.

On 30 May 1879 at Stafford House in London, Baroness Burdett-Coutts formed a separate Ladies' Committee consisting entirely of titled ladies, or as they were rather scathingly called 'the West End women'. They consisted of their Royal Highnesses, The Princess of Wales, Princess Christian, Duchess of Connaught, Duchess of Cambridge, Grand Duchess of Mecklemburg-Strelitz and Princess Mary (Duchess of Teck). Significantly, Lady Louise Wolseley, the beloved wife of the newly appointed Army Commander in South Africa, was persuaded to join, a strategically shrewd choice. The Ladies' Committee was backed up by forty-six titled gentlemen of wide influence.

They passed a resolution that deplored the lack of care provided for the wounded in Zululand. It was noted:

> As from the commencement of the outbreak of the war in Zululand no effort had been made on the part of any existing Society, or by any association of private individuals, to afford aid from England to our sick and wounded soldiers, sufferers in the above war.

A second meeting took place on 4 June when it was decided to dispatch trained nurses and a supply of medical comforts for the use of military hospitals. It was intended that the support would 'avoid collision or friction with the army medical staff'. So far, the British aid organizations had concerned themselves with wars involving other nations. Now, for the first time, they were proposing to send civilian nurses to help the hard-pressed British Army in South Africa. The British government remained wary about using civilian services, even though they thoroughly endorsed the work of the British Aid Society in foreign conflicts. The Army's Medical Department took the concept of female civilian nurses as a criticism of their capability and, predictably, such offers of help were stubbornly refused.

When Wolseley took over his South African command in July 1879, one of the many deficiencies he discovered was the desperate shortage of medical personnel in Natal. The large numbers of sick and wounded soldiers from the recently aborted invasion of Zululand highlighted the need for urgent additional help. Overcoming the objections of his Surgeon General, William Muir, Wolseley bowed to the gentle prompting of his wife and accepted the offer of help from the Stafford House South African Aid Committee. General Sir Henry Green, the committee's treasurer, had written to Wolseley asking how Stafford House could best help. The reply was a request for a modest number of personnel. Moving with great promptness, Baroness Burdett-Coutts was able to advise Wolseley that a party, including Sister Janet Wells, had already departed from London on 12 June bound for South Africa.

Sister Janet had been less than two months into her appointment in Newcastle when she received urgent notification that she had been especially selected by the committee to travel to South Africa. She was given just twenty-four hours' notice to journey to London to make her farewells and meet her companions at Paddington Station. There were just six other English nurses in the party. In overall command, with the title of Chief Commissioner, was Surgeon General (retired) James Tyrell Ross (see Appendix G), formerly of the Bengal Medical Department. During his thirty-five years' service in India he was involved in numerous campaigns and expeditions. Barely had he arrived back in England when he was invited to sit as a member of the Stafford House Committee where his immense experience was greatly valued and would contribute to the committee's success in South Africa. The second in command was a boisterous Irish surgeon named George Stoker, whose brother Bram would later gain immortality with his creation *Dracula*. George Stoker had served with the Stafford House Committee during the two Balkan Wars of 1876 and 1877–78. His superior officer during this period had been Vincent Kennet-Barrington, who left some unflattering opinions on Stoker's competence. It seems Stoker's knowledge of amputations did not stretch to the essential skills of tying arteries to prevent the patient bleeding to death. Now forbidden to operate, he spent his time treating fevers and dysentery. Kennet-Barrington had his own personal reason to question Stoker's credentials when he was nearly permanently blinded by an overdose of belladonna. He wrote:

> I was fool enough to have my eyes doctored by S (Stoker) who has partially blinded me. God knows when I shall get my sight back . . . God preserve me from the doctors out here.

Stoker's motive for volunteering for service in the earlier Balkan Wars had also been called into question. The main attraction was evidently the lure of the exotic East; he was known to be overly curious about harems and attractive slaves, tales of which he used to spice up his memoirs for his Victorian audiences. Nevertheless, Baroness Burdett-Coutts thought Stoker was invaluable as he was experienced and came from a solid Irish family. Stoker did outgrow this unpromising start to later hold many important posts, particularly specializing in problems of the throat, and became President of the British Laryngological Association, although it would appear that his strengths lay with organization rather than pure medicine.

Janet's family were stricken at the prospect of their young daughter again going into a dangerous war zone. South Africa was such a long way from home and the prospect of her facing the unknown dangers of disease and hostile natives filled them with great foreboding. They gained some comfort from the involvement of Lord Wolseley and his wife, whom they had met socially and at Court. The fact that Janet would be looking after British soldiers was also some consolation to the family. In spite of his fears for her safety, Benjamin Wells was very proud of his pretty young daughter and wrote a song for her.

The Red Cross Sister

The Red Cross sister sails over the Main,
On a mission of mercy, no greed of gain
Leaves Father and Mother and dearest friends
To succour the wounded the dying to tend.

Strong in her faith this sister so brave
Fears no danger wherever there's life to save
And when that's past hope she cheers their last breath
With the glorious promise of the life after death.

This Red Cross sister has powerful friends
Who vie with each other to further her ends
So when war and pestilence ravage the land
True charity comes from the Stafford House Band.

In spite of the shortage of time to prepare herself for such an epic journey, Janet managed to collect and pack the necessary items she knew from experience would be invaluable to her in the months ahead. Her faithful *kinjal* was carefully wrapped in a shawl and placed in the centre of her valise.

The nurses bound for South Africa were issued with a uniform by Stafford House which consisted of a black alpaca dress, a blue serge dress, a waterproof cloak, a pair of boots, a pair of shoes, and a full outfit of under-linen, aprons, and kerchiefs for a head-dress. As they were going into a war zone, it was considered appropriate to also issue them with a tropical helmet each, although this was not popular and was soon replaced by felt hats which they bought when they reached Durban. Each nurse was issued with an instrument case consisting of two subcutaneous injection syringes, two clinical thermometers, dressing and artery forceps, probes, directors and scissors. These nurses were expected to do much more than make beds, wash and care for the bodily needs of their patients. They were definitely not the usual concept of 'angels of mercy' handing out comforts and tucking in the odd bed sheet.

Janet's experience in the Russo-Turkish war was again invaluable to her and thanks to the generosity of her father, she was able to add to her instrument case a larger injection syringe for intramuscular injections, toothed and non-toothed dissecting forceps and a small collection of large and small scalpels. With her bible in one hand and *kinjal* in the other, she said she was ready for the challenge ahead. At the last moment her father gave her some sheets of his songs, which she tucked into her bag.

Janet's party travelled by train to the small Devon port of Dartmouth, where they were to catch the Donald Currie & Co. steam packet, the *Dublin Castle*, which was to be their home for the next six weeks.

Before embarking, Janet was required to sign her new conditions of employment:

Form of Agreement signed by the trained nurses engaged for service in South Africa under the Stafford House Committee

We – jointly and severally undertake and agree to proceed with all speed to South Africa, and to serve from the date of this agreement under the direction of the Surgeon General Ross, Commissioner of the Stafford House Committee, or his successor for the time being, and to proceed to such place or places and undertake such work and duties as we may jointly or severally be directed to do by the said Commissioner, and to perform the same to his entire satisfaction.

We, the said nurses, – jointly and severally undertake and agree to remain in South Africa, and work under the said Commissioner's direction for the space of six calendar months, unless prevented by certified ill-health or by some other cause which the said Commissioner shall accept as satisfactory. Provided always that in the event of cessation of hostilities the said Commissioner shall have the power to terminate our several engagements at any time within the said six months; and in the event of continuation of hostilities, we, the said nurses, severally undertake to continue our engagement as nurses for so long a period

81

exceeding the six months as our services may be required.

The agreement further witnesses that the undersigned Major General Sir H. Green, on behalf of the Stafford House Committee, agrees and undertakes to pay us, the said nurses, the sum of one pound per week, from the date of this agreement until our return to London; and further to provide during the continuance of this engagement, the said nurses with necessary food, outfit and travelling expenses*.

12th June 1879
Henry Green Major General
Hon. Treasurer, Stafford House South Africa Committee.

The *Dublin Castle* and her sister ships carrying the name *Castle* were employed during 1878–9 on the London to Cape Town route, conveying drafts of reinforcements to the Anglo Zulu War and returning with the sick and wounded bound for the main Army hospital at Netley in Hampshire. This was the start of the Union Castle Line, whose ships famously left Southampton at 4 p.m. every Thursday afternoon for the journey to the Cape until the 1960s.

Dartmouth, despite its small size, was a popular place to catch the Cape-bound ships because it cut out the tedium of embarking at Gravesend and sailing out of the Thames and along the south coast to Devon. At this stage of the war there was no further need of reinforcements and the passengers were mostly made up of civil servants, missionaries and traders. It was at this time that specially built troop-carrying ships came into service although scheduled passenger liners were still used to convey the larger drafts of troops. Mixing with the troops on long journeys was unpopular with the moneyed civilians travelling between South Africa and England; they liked their military to fight their wars as long as they did not have to have contact with them. In turn, the military, in the shape of the officers, found civilian shipmates

---

* Lodging, washing and clothing when required, might be added.

1. Sister Janet Wells, Royal Red Cross.

2. Janet's childhood home *(on left)* at 99 St Stephens Avenue, London *(Author's collection.)*

3. Sister Janet's mentor,
   Dr Laseron.
   (Sister Janet's scrapbook)

4. Protestant Deaconesses' training institute at Tottenham.

(Haringey Libraries, Archives and Museums)

5. A typical nursing ward at the hospital.   *(Haringey Libraries, Archives and Museums)*

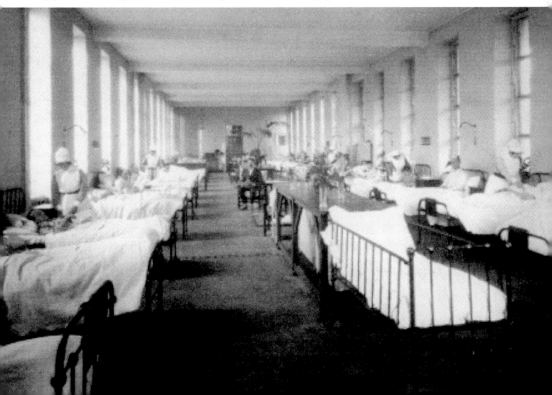

6. Sister Janet's passport dated 1877 which was issued to enable her to travel through Europe to Russia. It is endorsed by the Russian government. *(Sister Janet's scrapbook)*

7. Scutari hospital. *(Brian Best)*

8. Janet's route to the Russian front. The Sistova 'bridge of boats' across the Danube.
(Illustrated London News)

9. The *Dublin Castle.* The caption is in Janet's own handwriting. *(Sister Janet's scrapbook)*

*Sailed in her for the Seat of the Zulu War
June 13th 1879. from Dartmouth.*

10. A Natal mail cart, as used by Sister Janet to reach Utrecht. *(Illustrated London News)*

11. The original wagon route taken by Sister Janet en route to Pietermaritzburg. *(Adrian Greaves)*

12. One of many river obstacles en route to Utrecht. *(Adrian Greaves)*

Military Laager

13. Next to the hamlet of Utrecht was the army camp in which was located the wooden shed; the base hospital for the area. The caption is in Janet's own handwriting.

(Sister Janet's scrapbook)

14. Sister Janet attending the sick and wounded.   *(Sister Janet's scrapbook)*

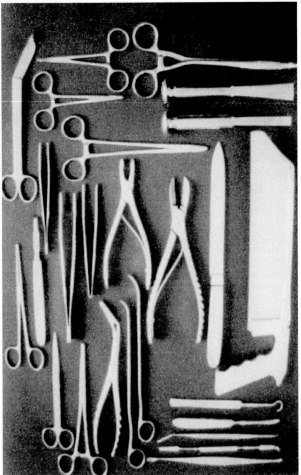

15. The contents of a South
    African field surgery kit,
    as used by Sister Janet.
    (Clifford Stossel)

16. Sister Janet administering
    to Trooper Harry
    Peterson. On the reverse
    was written:
*'Angels are painted fair to look
    like her
There's in her all that we believe
    of heaven
Amazing brightness, purity and
    truth
Eternal joy and everlasting love.
Harry Peterson.'*
        (Sister Janet's scrapbook)

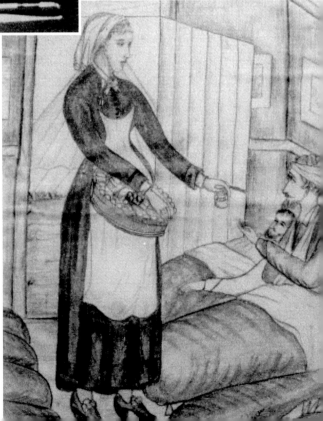

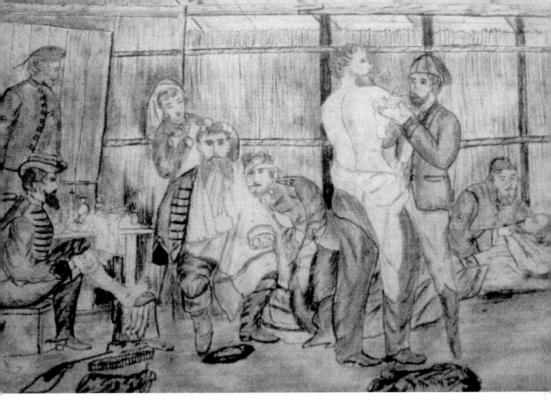

17. Sister Janet and Dr Fitzmaurice on duty in Utrecht hospital. *(Sister Janet's scrapbook)*

18. Camp Utrecht – the officers' mess of the 80 Regiment. The caption is in Janet's own handwriting. *(Sister Janet's scrapbook)*

Our Mess hut at Rorkes Drift

19. Sister Janet's Zulu hut at Rorke's Drift. The battlefield is in the background. The caption is in Janet's own handwriting. *(Sister Janet's scrapbook)*

20. The Coghill and Melvill memorial. The caption is in Janet's own handwriting. *(Sister Janet's scrapbook)*

Lieutenants Melville and Coghills graves who fell Jan. 22nd 1879

21. Flowers and ferns collected at the memorial to Coghill and Melvill by Janet for her scrapbook.
(Sister Janet's scrapbook)

22. Items collected for her scrapbook at Isandlwana. The entries are in Janet's handwriting.
(Sister Janet's scrapbook)

23. Isandlwana before the Zulu attack. *(Sister Janet's scrapbook)*

24. A modern view of Isandlwana and cairns. *(Adrian Greaves)*

25. Lord Chelmsford's (and Sister Janet's) picnic rock at Mangeni waterfall.

(David Rattray)

26. Durban in 1879. *(Author's collection)*

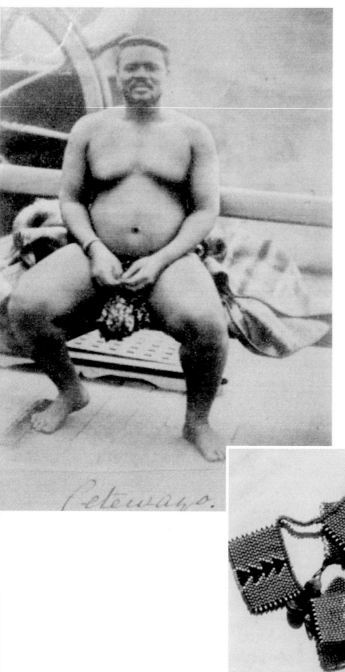

Cetewayo.

27. King Cetshwayo. The caption is in Janet's own handwriting. _(Sister Janet's scrapbook)_

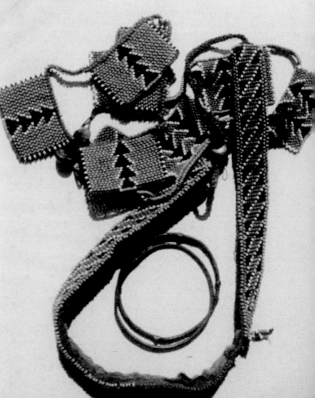

28. Beads given to Sister Janet by King Cetshwayo. _(AZWHS)_

29. Janet's husband, George King.
(Sister Janet's scrapbook)

30. Nurse Janet Wells, aged nineteen, from
her parents' cameo brooch.   *(AZWHS)*

31. Sister Janet's medals and uniform buttons. Medals left to right: Russian Inperial Order of
the Red Cross; The Royal Red Cross; The South Africa Campaign medal.   *(AZWHS)*

32. Sister Janet meeting Lord Roberts, Commander-in-Chief, at Queen Victoria's funeral.
(Sister Janet's scrapbook

33. The last picture taken of Sister Janet, aged fifty-three.

34. The grave of Sister Janet in Purley.
(Brian Best

THE LATE MRS. GEORGE KING.
(Who, as "Sister Janet," did such valuable work during the Russo-Turkish War.)

rather ordinary and below their station as they did not share their narrow interests in hunting and regimental affairs. A mutual contempt kept the military and civilians apart and there was little fraternization.The medical party was the exception to this rule as many of them were not only the officers' social equals, but also shared a common bond in the care of both the officers and their men. A junior officer of the Royal Artillery, Lieutenant Henry Curling, who had earlier sailed to Cape Town on the *Dublin Castle*, wrote this description of the vessel in one of his many letters home:

> This is a very fine steamer (3,000 tons) and the cabins are very comfortable though not equal to P. & O. boats. The food is good but quite the steamer kind. The steamer is one of those tremendously long ones being rigged with red and black funnels that you often see passing Ramsgate. She is very low in the water so does not roll too much. There are no bulwarks, only rails which made it bitterly cold on deck.

Janet thought the boat very splendid, its long low lines and the open rails gave the vessel the appearance of an elegant greyhound of the seas. Although the open rails aesthetically pleased her artistic eye in port, once they reached the open sea she was to regret the lack of the shelter of the solid bulwarks common to other vessels.

Janet was fortunate to be allocated a small cabin to herself. It was half the size of a normal two-berth cabin, the other half being taken up by stores of lifebelts and spare seat squabs. She really did not mind the smallness of the cabin, she was just very grateful to have some time on her own after the rush of the previous few days. She was relieved to see the bunk had a rail along the side to prevent her from rolling out of bed in rough weather, although waking in the night in the confined space of the bunk reminded her of the graves she and her fellow nurses had slept in for safety during the Balkan war. The results of the horrors and extremes of endurance they suffered during that conflict would follow Janet and her companions for many years.

The voyage was broken by stops at Gibraltar, to deliver mail and orders to the garrison commander and to allow staff to tranship to the Mediterranean ports of Valetta and Alexandria, and then Madeira, to take on provisions before the long trip down the west coast of Africa.

The Victorians enjoyed their musical evenings and the master of the *Dublin Castle*, Captain M.H. Penfold, encouraged his officers to contribute to these affairs. Being an accomplished musician with an extensive repertoire, Janet became a great favourite at these impromptu concerts. Janet, like many young Victorian ladies, kept a scrapbook and had started a new one for her South African venture. One of the early items pasted on its pages was a patriotic song she performed during the voyage, which was typical of the period, being not only jingoistic and stirring but also factually inaccurate.

The Royal 24th

As sung on board the R.M.S. *Dublin Castle*
on Tuesday July 1, 1879
To the Air – *My Grandfather's Clock*. Written by Janet Wells

I'm the chip off a block, who has stood like a rock
Through many a long campaign
Mid the heaviest of fire, he would never retire,
Though his comrades in thousands were slain
He belongs to the corps, of the brave "twenty four"
Who so gallantly marched side by side
'Till they stood – fell – never to march again
And like heroes died.

Chorus
Only six hundred numbering – Howard's fine corps
In death now slumbering, brave 24th
They stood – fast – never to march again
And like heroes died.

84

One man near the camp, at the dawning of the day
The sentinels paced to and fro,
And soon they espied, rushing down the hill side
In thousands the wild shrieking foe,
Not a man left his post, but confronted the host,
And they fought with true British pride
'Till they stood – fast – never to march again
And like heroes died.

Chorus

Though wonders were done against forty to one,
And the Zulus fell round them like hail
Though retreat was cut off and their last hope was gone
Not a heart in the regiment would quail,
Like lions they fought and no quarter was sought
'Till outnumbered on every side
They fell – fast – never to rise again
And like heroes died.

Chorus

Some few cut their way through the thick of the fray
And with Bromhead returned to the camp
Their numbers were few (eighty men staunch and true)
But no forces their courage could damp
Though fierce the attack 'twas at length beated back
By these brave men who legions defied;
For they stood – fast – and fired to the last
As their comrades died.

Chorus

But eighty men numbering – brave four score
Their comrades slumbering brave 'twenty four'
They stood – fast – and fired to the last
As their comrades died.

CHAPTER NINE

Arrival in South Africa

After several stormy weeks the *Dublin Castle* finally docked at Cape Town. Janet and her party had found the previous weeks at sea increasingly boring and were very glad to disembark to take in the local sights. Cape Town was already showing signs of development from the rather sleepy backwater that Lieutenant Curling had found the previous year. With the expansion of the diamond fields to the distant north and the commercial possibilities opening in post-war Natal, the port had become a magnet for those seeking their fortune.

Chief Commissioner Ross called on Lady Frere, in her capacity as the Cape Town representative of the Stafford House South Africa Aid Committee, to learn what had been done so far and to discover where help was most needed. It was clear from her report that the military were still reluctant to accept civilian nurses, although some Sisters of Charity, from Bloemfontein in the Transvaal, were employed at the hospital in Ladysmith. He learned that everyday supplies were short so, before he left, Ross managed to organize an on-going supply to be sent from the Cape to Natal that included cows, goats and poultry. Most foods considered necessary for the sick and wounded, like milk and eggs, were outrageously expensive and almost unprocurable in Natal. The Castle Line's owner, Donald Currie, readily volunteered that supplies for the Stafford House nurses would be carried free of charge on his vessels.

After a short but interesting stay, Janet and her fellow nurses left Cape Town on the 8 July 1879 and sailed along the east coast to the main Natal port of Durban. They arrived off Durban on 12 July but had to wait until the 14th for the heavy sea to moderate before they could be taken across the notorious sand bar that was such an inconvenience to all who arrived by sea. Ross had managed to reach the shore on a mail boat two days earlier and had been able to make arrangements for the dispersal of his staff. Once they were able to land, the nurses were split up into pairs with the exception of Sister Janet, who was considered, at just nineteen years of age, the most experienced.

Remaining in Durban were Sisters Ruth and Elizabeth. Sisters Mary and Annette went to Pietermaritzburg, while Sisters Emma and Edith travelled to Ladysmith. It was just as well that Sister Janet was the most experienced and resourceful of all, as she had to make her own way to the remote border settlement of Utrecht, where the hospital that supported Sir Evelyn Wood's northern column was located. Janet was delighted to be chosen to go to Utrecht, even though the prospect of a long and difficult journey across over 220 miles of uninhabited African bush was somewhat daunting. This posting to Utrecht would be Janet's first experience of nursing British soldiers and she relished the prospect of both the long journey and caring for patients from home.

The only means of getting the nurses to their various destinations was by the daily mail cart, drawn by two horses. This bone-shaking form of transport was regarded as both unsafe and unsuitable for passengers, especially ladies, but with no other alternative available Ross, Sisters Edith, Emma and Janet set off for Ladysmith in their respective carts. Little did the nurses know that, apart from the rough but well used dirt roadway to Pietermaritzburg, there were only rough tracks to take them beyond to their various destinations – these rutted dirt tracks were frequently criss-crossed by cattle tracks which made their route across the sparsely populated rolling hills and bush confusing and very tricky to navigate. And then there were the fearsome dried river beds (*dongas*) with their steep crumbling sides and fast flowing rivers to be negotiated.

From Durban, they commenced the long steady ten mile climb away from the hot tropical-like heat of the coast. The lush leafy trees overhung the track and the ever present monkeys and baboons kept up their incessant warning cries as the carts lumbered up the long haul to the hilly range that would lead them on to Pietermaritzburg. Once away from the heat of the coast the temperature became more pleasant and the thick trees gave way to rolling hills with scattered kraals and homesteads dotted across the open countryside. Owing to transport difficulties, the Army having commandeered every available wagon, there were no fresh horses available so the party were kept at Pieter-maritzburg until 18 July. They did not reach Ladysmith until the 20th due to a delay of twenty hours because, when horses had been found, they were unfit for the task of running the post carts and had to be walked. After dropping off Sisters Edith and Emma at the British garrison of Ladysmith at 4 p.m., Sister Janet immediately continued her arduous journey. By now Janet was getting familiar with the never ending hills to be crossed, to the young nurse they seemed to go on forever and there was little to distract her – apart from the well rutted track that would regularly cause the wagon to get stuck or jolt with such force that she was acquiring an impressive number of bruises. They eventually reached the outpost of Newcastle the following evening at 8 p.m. where she rested in a local inn for the night. She wrote in her diary 'after an unsafe journey'.

Starting early the following morning, her driver was able to make better time as the track was infrequently used and in better condition. The track to Utrecht took them along a thirty-five mile valley until a large hill with two smaller satellite hills came into view. Her guide became volubly excited and Janet realized that her long journey was nearly complete.

Despite the uncomfortable bone-shaking motion of the mail cart, Janet had been totally captivated by the sheer beauty and scope of the vast veld. One year earlier she had crossed the barren plains of the Balkan countries but the wide, sweeping, empty countryside of this virtually unexplored land was stunningly beautiful. Janet's 200 plus mile journey had been tiring and occasionally painful; travelling in an unsprung mail cart on rutted and badly pot-holed tracks had necessitated her being strapped into her seat during the last part of the journey to prevent her being thrown about. It was just as well; so bad were the tracks on the final five miles leading to Utrecht that the over-excited Boer driver managed to overturn the cart in his enthusiasm to complete the journey. It could have been worse. As it was, Janet was trapped beneath the cart and it took the driver a good five minutes to free her before they could right the cart itself.

Nevertheless, now bruised, battered and bloodied after her long and arduous journey, Janet was thrilled to be approaching Utrecht. Situated in a strongly Boer area near the border of the Transvaal and northern Zululand, this was one of the remotest and most hostile areas of northern Natal and a region still regarded as dangerous due to bands of marauding Zulus. She arrived at the settlement of Utrecht late on the evening of 22 July, fortunate to escape with only grazes and heavy bruising to her shoulder and left arm. Chief Commissioner Ross later wrote in his report:

Sister Janet showed great pluck and endurance on this journey of five consecutive days by mail cart, 217 miles were gone over; but it was rough and severe travelling; and the vehicle was upset on the way. At this town a room has been engaged for the Sister in the house of the only English family in the place. On the 23rd she entered on her work at the hospital.

The weather during her journey had been dry with bright blue skies and warm sunshine during the day, but was very cold and almost frosty at night, typical of winter in the high veld country. Nightfall comes very quickly and the wide sweeping brown plains of dried grass are instantly transformed into inky darkness as the sun drops suddenly below the distant horizon. Janet was pleased to have the warm waterproof cape as part of her Stafford House uniform.

The settlement, for it was hardly a town, had at its centre a court-house, a hotel that sold questionable gin out of teacups, a general store, a chapel and about twenty houses. The region was remote, well watered and spacious, offering the ideal home for the pioneering community; it also felt safe, surrounded by hills less than two miles away. Janet's Boer guide warned her that the local Utrecht people were staunch Boers and republican to a man, and all fiercely resented the British presence. For a short while during the 1850s the area had declared itself an independent republic named after the settlement of Utrecht in Holland, and meaning 'the outside meadow', but its small size, just twenty-five miles wide and forty miles long, and the constant clashes with its Zulu neighbours, eventually drove the fledgling republic into the protective arms of the British, who were tolerated by the Boers – for the time being. Despite a number of serious raids from the local Zulu tribe, led by Prince Mbelini, the Boers could not bring themselves to form an alliance with the British, whose motives they distrusted. Only one Boer leader from Utrecht, Piet Uys, had offered his services and brought forty of his family with him as irregular cavalry. Sadly, Uys and many of his followers were killed during the chaotic retreat following the recent and doomed British attack against the Zulus at Hlobane Mountain.

Meanwhile, the sending of the civilian Stafford House nurses to aid the British troops in Zululand had been widely reported in the British press and seriously embarrassed the Army authorities into sending a party of their own nurses from the Army's Royal Victoria Hospital at Netley. Stafford House had let it be known that their nurses were proving beyond doubt the value of women as war nurses. The press reported tales of the Stafford House nurses' pluck, long journeys over rough country, upset mail carts, falls from horseback and so on, all calculated to challenge the male stereotype that nurses were of no use in warfare. Clearly embarrassed by the advantage gained by the civilian nurses, the Army acted: led by Jane Deeble, six nurses were duly sent to Natal and arrived a month after the Stafford House contingent. This prompted a stuffy comment by William Muir, the Director General of the Army Medical Department to Netley's administrator:

I hope the exodus of Mrs. Deeble & Co. won't much dislocate your Hospital arrangements. The ladies in the West End (Stafford House) have gone mad as to nursing and other aid for our poor fellows at the Cape, and the Govt. felt bound to be a match for them. As to the wisdom of the step we have our own doubts and misgivings.

Florence Nightingale was distinctly unimpressed by Mrs Deeble but tried to be fair and wrote that she was:

> . . . brave, sincere and courageous, but had no observation and was incapable of understanding, far less of making a regulation or organization. She will be engaged in arranging a 'nice tea' for the Nurses while she lets the Nursing go to ruin. – I have not approached the subject of the Regulations yet with Mrs Deeble.
>
> I doubt whether she has seen them. I doubt whether she is able to understand them. I doubt whether she has a glimmer of the fact that she is to have a personal relationship with and report to the War Office.

The Military Nursing Service was born after a long and difficult labour. In 1861 Florence Nightingale had recommended Jane Shaw Stewart, the aristocratic daughter of Sir Michael Shaw Stewart, 6th Baronet of Ardgowan to the post of Superintendent of Nurses at the Woolwich Hospital. She moved to Netley on 25 May 1868. After a very unhappy and tempestuous period, when the autocratic Jane Shaw Stewart attempted to impose her will on the Military Nursing Service, the War Office instituted an enquiry into the conduct of the Superintendent General of Nursing at Netley and the bad state of nursing. The setting up of the enquiry was the culmination of the continuous series of claims, counter claims, accusations and recriminations that had accompanied Jane Shaw Stewart's career in Military General Hospitals. Colonel Wilbraham, the Military Governor, expressed the opinion that she exhibited a violent temper, and an imperious and inflammatory manner, which provoked complaints from nurses, orderlies, medical officers and even patients.

Florence Nightingale believed Jane Stewart's hints that some of Colonel Wilbraham's resentments originated outside the hospital. He felt maligned when the aristocratic Superintendent

General declined to socialize with his sisters or accept their vague offers of help on the wards.

The War Office produced a report that was not communicated to either Colonel Wilbraham or Jane Shaw Stewart. They were both sent a private letter of reprimand. More seriously, she failed to reach agreement with the Medical Officers at both Netley and Woolwich and the nurses were unable to carry out many of their duties. As she became more isolated and unable to carry out her duties, or communicate with the Medical Staff, she resigned to be replaced by Mrs Jane Deeble, the widow of an Army Medical Officer.

Others saw the case very differently. The medical officers had secured the replacement of the haughty Mrs Stewart by a woman of their own class. Mrs Deeble's failings, her homeliness, her lack of interest in constitutional rights and wrongs were exactly the qualities admired by her male and female colleagues alike. Her appointment guaranteed the survival of the female Military Nursing Service, although not in its original form. Despite opposition from the pioneer of military nursing, the formidable Mrs Deeble remained Nursing Superintendent at Netley for many years. By the time the Netley group arrived in South Africa they had heard tales of the hardships that their rivals, the Stafford House nurses, endured in reaching their destinations and the Netley nurses were determined to match them for hardiness. (See Appendix C)

Sister Emma Durham, the Stafford House nurse who had been assigned to Ladysmith, amusingly recalled that in order to assist Mrs Deeble's party, she had sought out and prepared rooms for the newcomers only for Mrs Deeble to stoically decline a roof over their heads and insist that they too would live under canvas. Brave Mrs Deeble; her nurses were unused to erecting tents and all offers of help were refused by the stern matron. To the amusement of onlookers, unused to seeing ladies erect large and heavy tents, the effort took a good hour before their two tents took on a recognizable but precarious shape. Meanwhile, unnoticed by Mrs Deeble, the daily thunderstorm gathered menacingly over Ladysmith. With the nurses' tents in the process of being haphazardly pitched, and with their luggage still in the open wagon, the rainsquall and high winds suddenly arrived. Within seconds a heavy, noisy and very severe thunderstorm flattened their tents, which terrified and drenched the startled nurses. A bedraggled Mrs Deeble had the presence of mind to get her soaked and shivering party into their wagon, which was urgently driven back the quarter-mile into the centre of Ladysmith where Sister Durham, who had already received accounts of the event, was waiting for them; she led them in to their dry lodgings. After just this single experience, which was no worse than any thunderstorm at that time of year, Mrs Deeble announced the entire Netley team would return to civilized Durban. They departed the following morning where they thereafter staffed the main hospital from their safe and comfortable quarters.

CHAPTER TEN

Utrecht: every officer rose
to his feet . . .

Meanwhile, the battle-weary British forces at Utrecht had very warmly received Sister Janet. Janet was delighted to learn that she would be lodged with the only English family in the nearby hamlet and on her arrival at the house she was led off by her hostess to her room and a much appreciated hot bath. Janet later remembered that she undressed and slipped into the hot water with a deep sigh of relief. This was the first time she had been able to wash or change her clothes for five days. The housemaid carried off her dusty clothes for washing and Janet was able to anoint her bruises with arnica.

Dressing quickly, Janet went to join her host family for a welcome evening meal. She had so many questions to ask but her new friends, who had not had news from Durban or the nearby village of Newcastle for some time, were eager to hear all the latest news and gossip; they bombarded Janet with their questions. After an excellent meal and drowsy from the fatigue of her travels and a blazing fire, Janet bade her kind hosts good-night and retired to her comfortable bed. Before she slipped into a dreamless sleep, she recalled how her mind wandered over the work that lay before her. The family had warned her that malaria was rife in the area and that many soldiers suffered and died of the disease without knowing they were carrying the malarial parasite. She would soon come face to face with the unpleasant side effects that included fever, rupture of the spleen, anaemia and an impaired immune system which would leave her patients open to the endemic diseases such as typhus, influenza, dysentery and malnutrition.

Janet's concerned hosts also warned her of the local common gossip that syphilis caused more soldiers to seek medical help than any other ailment apart from battle wounds. She quickly discovered the condition was considered by the soldiers to be 'part of life' though to the medical officers it posed a serious problem, as sufferers were frequently unable to perform their duty due to raging headaches, swollen joints, lesions, sores and ulcers. Janet knew from her work in London that the only treatment available to her was bismuth, which certainly was no cure, and the long-term prognosis was death, as and when major organs and blood vessels became affected. From her conversation with her hosts, Janet had been surprised to learn that tuberculosis was prevalent among the soldiers; she had previously seen a great deal of the disease among the malnourished and poverty stricken slum dwellers round London.

Ironically, many of the soldiers had joined the Army to escape the poverty and squalor at home, only to contract disease in the vastness of South Africa. Chelmsford's whole force had frequently been forced to shelter in hastily prepared and cramped fortifications and, by living in squalid and overcrowded conditions, the disease soon became rife.

The next morning, dressed in her long dark blue dress and white headdress with an armband bearing the red cross and the letters 'S.H.', and carrying her white apron, Sister Janet proudly reported for duty at the makeshift hospital, which she discovered was well established and in good condition, being protected by an outer barricade in the event of a Zulu attack. The hospital consisted of a substantial wooden single storey structure situated just inside the main defensive laager of marquee and bell tents. Like many settlements of Dutch influence, Utrecht was built in a long broad valley; the settlement bounded by the Langabalele range of hills on one side and the Piet Uys hills on the other. The total civilian population was just under 300 souls, mostly Dutch Boers.

Surgeon Major J. Fitzmaurice was already waiting at the hospital hut for Janet. He watched the slim pretty girl, smart as a new pin in her crisply starched and ironed uniform, and smiled to himself; the early morning breeze had ruffled her unruly hair which had, as usual, escaped from the restraint of her cap. Having read the report that accompanied Sister Janet he knew what a selfless, courageous and resourceful girl she was, from both the account of her service with the Russians and of her hazardous journey from Durban. He reckoned she would be more than a match for his wary Army medical team and the soldiers who would be under her care. He introduced her to the male medical orderlies, recruited from the camp's soldiers, who greeted her courteously but their scepticism about her abilities, and the suitability of a young English nurse in the harsh environment of a military hospital, was obvious in their manner. She offered the committee funds to Major Fitzmaurice but he was happy for Janet to take charge of the account, which she would use to supply extra comforts for the patients. There were eighty-eight patients in the hospital and another twenty-nine were due to arrive from Ulundi that afternoon. Sister Janet noted that she was 'immediately immersed in much busy work'.

She quickly settled in and swiftly proved she was both talented and highly trained and by the end of the week the doctors were delighted to leave the running of the hospital in her capable hands. After her dreadful experience in the Russo-Turkish War she noted that, 'It was a delightful pleasure to nurse the English soldiers'.

During her first week the winter sun was still comfortably hot and the sky a clear brilliant blue. The brown parched veld stretched into a seemingly infinite distance; the blueness of the distant haze made her think of the sea. Janet wrote that winter in South Africa, despite the chilly temperatures at night, was certainly very pleasant and comfortable.

Equally, Janet was certainly a most welcome sight for the wounded and sick patients who filled the wards. Apart from her nursing care and feminine presence, they loved any little luxury she could obtain for them: sometimes a rare tin of jam, some pipe tobacco or a little butter, which, due to the shortage of supplies, then cost an exorbitant 10s 6d per lb. These she would buy from the trading wagons whenever they visited the camp. Every Sunday, she accompanied the chaplain at the head of the church parade. There was a church room adjoining White's Stores and she attended the daily services and sang in the choir when her duties allowed. During the evenings she often sat with the seriously ill patients and quietly read requested passages from the Bible. The not so ill patients would also try to persuade her to sit and read to them, but she was fully aware that it was definitely not the passages from the Bible that interested them.

The defeat of the Zulus at the recent battle of Ulundi left the hospital brim full of soldiers suffering from battle wounds and general sickness. Each day brought more casualties that were grievously injured or seriously ill from a variety of medical conditions. There were also many soldiers who had been in the hospital for a considerable time. Most of these men had been fighting during the hot summer months of the rainy season, so the troops had to endure both rainstorms and blistering heat; dehydration and heat exhaustion also badly affected the unsuitably clothed men. Heavy serge jackets and trousers in dark colours severely hampered those working in high temperatures and it would be another twenty years before lightweight tropical kit would be issued for hot climates.

Blisters caused by marching in heavy steel-shod boots affected the efficiency of just about every soldier, except, of course, the officers, who had their uniforms and boots specially made for them at considerable personal expense. Blisters frequently became infected and Janet and her orderlies regularly de-roofed the blisters and cleansed and dressed the suppurating sores with salt. They often said that if they had a shilling for every pair of feet treated for blisters they would be able to retire to a mansion by the sea. The soldiers were highly amused by Janet's remedy for the rotting fungal disease that seriously affected their feet, a scourge that afflicted soldiers in any hot climate. She instructed them to urinate in their boots each evening, and then let the boots dry out overnight. Janet knew the urea in the urine would kill off the fungus; to the soldiers it was a miracle cure.

Marching through torrential rainstorms, wading across

97

swollen streams and sleeping in wet clothes led to an enormous increase in the number of soldiers suffering from rheumatism, for which there was no treatment, leaving the sufferer crippled. Many of the ordinary soldiers had infections in childhood that had damaged their joints. Eventually they were unable to soldier on and were discharged as medically unfit. Janet wrote that she felt desperately sorry for these poor fellows who were in constant and severe pain, often worsened by debilitating fever. Gently she applied cold compresses to the red-hot swollen joints and fevered foreheads to try to ease their pain and lower their fever before they were shipped back to England and a desperately uncertain future.

Janet had quickly discovered that the average British soldier was not a physically impressive specimen when initially recruited, though after two years campaigning in South Africa they had become a hardy and seasoned force. In spite of the 1874 reforms, that had been introduced by Edward Cardwell, Secretary for War, to improve conditions by reducing the enlistment period to six years in the hope of attracting a higher calibre of recruit, the standard continued to fall. The average height for a soldier was 5 feet 8 inches in 1870, which dropped to 5 feet 4 inches by the outbreak of the Zulu War in 1879. The stunted development and poor physical state of many of these men usually resulted from a deprived and miserable environment. Their condition left them prey to catching the many diseases that were rife in the tropics. Common day-to-day illnesses that afflicted the British soldier included influenza which, though not usually a killer, frequently developed into pneumonia which was often fatal. The only treatment available for bacterial or viral pneumonia was excellent nursing care. As much nourishment as it was possible to obtain or to persuade the patient to take was one remedy of the time, as a proper diet could improve resistance to the infection, along with tepid sponging and application of cold compresses to reduce the fever. Eucalyptus inhalations and massaging the patient's back would also help to relieve congested lungs. A native plant, the *khathazo,* was used as it was found to be useful in treating both influenza and pneumonia by acting as an expectorant that eased the lung congestion causing the breathing problems.

Local remedies used by the Boer and Zulu people at Utrecht could treat many other complaints and Janet was always prepared to try them on her patients. Severe sunburn was effectively treated by a generous application of the juice from crushed aloe. These strange, almost cacti-like plants grew in profusion all over the area. Janet was very interested in local remedies, many of which were highly efficacious. Dr Laseron's beginnings with his pharmacy in Tottenham, including the use of unconventional remedies, had ensured that his nurses had as much knowledge as possible of pharmacology, 'tablets, powders, lotions and potions' as Janet and her fellow trainees called his lectures, and he had never deprecated local remedies.

To familiarize Janet, Surgeon Major Fitzmaurice gave her a document to read entitled *Report on the climate and Diseases of Natal and Zululand*, which the Army Medical Department issued in September 1878:

> Dysentery is not very common, but the occurrence of bloody urine is very frequent in both man and animals, and tapeworm exists to such an extent that Dr. Jones says, 'almost every second person you meet with has worms of some sort'. The water in this locality is slightly brackish, but not apparently productive of any injury to health. On the whole, Dr. Jones regards the Lower Tugela division as being 'remarkably healthy'.

With respect to the climate and diseases of the Upper Tugela between Umsinga and the river, Dr Dalzell, district surgeon, looked on fever as comparatively rare, never having seen any serious cases except those brought out of north Zululand:

> The high lands are remarkably healthy. It is likely that white men living in the deep valleys would take fever, but no white men live there. Dysentery and rheumatism appear to be more common in this locality, where also tapeworm exists 'in abundance'.
>
> Cases of sunstroke have occurred, and Dr. Dalzell speaks of the heat in the valleys during the summer months as

'terrible' between the hours of 11 and 3 p.m., also the Tugela (18 or 20 miles only from this) runs in a deep valley. Troops could not easily be kept healthy there, owing to the intense heat, while horses would almost inevitably die in great numbers unless stabled.

Janet quickly realized the significance of references to worms and tapeworms, which she suspected infected a number of her new patients. Knowing that infestations of worms were a major cause of malnutrition, the young nurse set about preparing an armoury of remedies to combat them. First she went to the nearby stream, a tributary of the Sand River, which provided water for the camp and its hospital. Being the dry winter season the water level was low, but as she walked upstream she saw the bodies of two dead cattle and the signs of the men's indiscriminate ablutions in the water. She had found the cause of many of the cases of dysentery and camp fever in the hospital. Next she went to see the commissary who was responsible for the stores, to enquire about the source and cooking of the meat in camp. Anyone who knew Janet of old could have warned the unsuspecting commissary officer that, despite her soft voice and gentle smile, when Janet's jaw was set forward and square, she was quite implacable and would not have disgraced any famous warrior in her battle for her patients.

Fortunately he was a sensible chap and listened carefully to what Janet had to say. Janet recalled that she protested that the water carts used for collecting water were lined with mould and smelled offensive; she also pointed out that the soldiers would not boil their water and gave the excuse that it 'tasted funny'. He agreed that in future he would ensure the water supply from the river would be kept unsullied and boiled before distribution; the meat would likewise be well cooked to kill any worms residing therein. With these simple measures in force, there was an immediate decrease in cases of dysentery and typhoid fever.

Any patients found to have worms were given a concoction of sodium sulphate, sodium citrate and bicarbonate of soda, which Janet flavoured with glycerine and aniseed to hide the disagreeable taste. Copious quantities of salt and water were also given to flush the resultant debris from the system. The rest of the patients were given a dose of castor oil or Epsom salts, 'just in case'. Sadly there was no known cure for tapeworms and the patient would eventually die when the worm infected the brain. Janet wrote to her fellow nurses in Durban, Pietermaritzburg and Ladysmith about her findings in Utrecht and Surgeon General Ross found the requests for castor oil, Epsom salts and the soda concoction suddenly rising.

Janet not only had to look after the camp hospital, but was also required to ride out to the outlying camps, often inside Zululand, to attend the sick and wounded. Some years before, Janet had ridden a horse in London but riding for miles over open veld on an Army horse, regardless of the attempt by the stables to find her the most docile mount, bore little resemblance to a gentle trot round the rides in the park near her home. To assist her, a farrier sergeant had roughly converted a military saddle into a ladies' side-saddle. Due to the rough ground around Utrecht, riding side-saddle was too dangerous so she quickly adapted to riding in the soldiers' style using a conventional saddle. The 80th (Staffordshire) Regiment was the unit which had been based at Luneberg to the north of Utrecht and had taken part in the advance on Ulundi. They had left behind some scattered detachments to keep an eye on the more militant Zulu clans. The area was still the most sensitive in Zululand, with the Zulu Prince Mbelini still defiant and threatening revenge; another chief, Manyanyoba, continued to be a threat to Utrecht and its surrounding area.

Sporadic outbreaks of fighting continued with bands of rebellious warriors attacking patrols. On one occasion a guide with one of these patrols raced into the hospital with the news that a marauding band had attacked the patrol and there were several casualties who had taken refuge in a cave in the direction of the Bevana River. With the only two available doctors in the midst of surgery, Janet packed a medical kit and, accompanied by an orderly and an armed escort, set out on the ten-mile ride to help the casualties. Several anxious faces greeted them as they rode up to the cave. Dismounting from her horse, Janet hurried to aid the injured men. Fortunately, most of the wounds were superficial and although they had bled profusely the injuries were not immediately life threatening. The orderly began to cleanse and dress these wounds while Janet dealt with the one severely injured soldier.

The man, Joseph Legg, had a bullet wound in the shoulder and an assegai spear wound to his thigh. The bullet was still lodged in his shoulder and the jagged entry wound was already looking red and angry. Janet knew she had to remove the bullet if the man was to stand any chance of survival, and without anaesthetic the operation would be a severe trial for both of them. Janet assembled her instruments and, after giving Joseph a dose of laudanum to dull the pain called the guide and a soldier to hold the poor man firmly. She cleansed the wound with antiseptic and thanking God that she did not have to extend the wound, slipped the toothed dissecting forceps into the gaping hole and, firmly gripping the round bullet, smoothly withdrew it. Fortunately at that moment Joseph fainted and while he was unconscious Janet finished dressing the wound with a tenax dressing, made of waterproof flax impregnated with herbs, which she bandaged firmly into place. The assegai wound was simpler to deal with as the blade had not hit any major blood vessel or damaged the muscle and, once cleaned and dressed, Janet felt sure it would heal without too much difficulty. A few hours later a relief party with a cart arrived from the hospital and Janet was able to transfer her wounded soldiers to the safety of the hospital.

On one occasion, when she was on her rounds of the scattered camps, Janet and her guide were late returning to camp when they realized a party of possibly hostile Zulus was resting between them and the camp. Unnoticed by the Zulus, Janet and her guide were forced to hide in the bush. Shades of Vardin she later recalled as, *kinjal* in hand, and wrapped in her long warm cloak, she and the guide curled up in a *donga* (a dry river bed) which, in the dry winter season, was full of rough scrub and large rocks. By the following dawn the Zulus had already moved away and Janet and her guide were able to continue on their rounds.

The area was finally made safe when men of Colonel Baker Russell's Flying Column attacked the Zulu chief Manyanyoba's caves overlooking the Ntombe River.

102

Lieutenant Henry Curling wrote home describing this final act of the Anglo Zulu War:

> There is a small tribe here living in some caves that overlook the road, who will not submit. They have continued to fire on everybody passing by and have prevented any small parties from moving about. The first day we came here we surrounded their caves and summoned them to surrender. Eight of them came out with their arms and gave themselves up. Unfortunately, some of our own men were fired upon from another cave and our own niggers immediately assegaied the prisoners. The others then refused to come out.
>
> Large fires were lit at the mouth of the cave to smoke them out, but without avail. We have been here 3 days and they will not give in so, as we are to move tomorrow and this nest of vipers cannot be left here, the caves are to be blown up with gun-cotton. We are expecting to hear the explosion every minute. It seems cruel but must be done.

With her cheerful efficiency, Sister Janet became a firm favourite with her patients and she was generally and affectionately referred to as 'Little Sister'. She enjoyed attending the officers' mess for dinner and was filled with pride and pleasure as every officer rose to his feet as she entered. In fact it took no time at all for the pretty young nurse to overcome any resentment that may have lingered about civilians being foisted on the military – especially when Surgeon Major Fitzmaurice let it be known that she had previously served with the Russian army in the Balkan War.

The story of Janet's near encounter with the Zulu war party improved with each telling and the officers, who were all very keen to see the famous *kinjal*, gently teased her. Her courage and resourcefulness in the treatment and care of the wounded soldiers near the Bevana River, while not abating the teasing over the *kinjal*, did raise their admiration and respect for her both as a nurse and a human being.

Janet took all this in good part and returned their teasing with equal measure. She spiritedly retorted that she regretted having

103

to leave her club behind, as she was sure it would be 'useful bludgeoning some of the blockheads in camp'. Coming from a large happy family, the experience of her childhood made her duties easy for her and the 'boys' in camp quickly became her 'family'. Her cheerful, kindly and efficient personality brightened up the dull and remote post and she enjoyed great popularity among the staff and patients alike.

CHAPTER ELEVEN

So many frightening
diseases . . .

and wounds for a young nurse to treat . . .

W hen Sister Janet travelled to South Africa, malaria was virtually extinct in the United Kingdom, but the disease continued to be a serious health hazard for the British Army in Africa. Referring to the Anglo Zulu War, the *History of the Army Medical Department* records that malaria and bowel diseases were the most serious medical problems facing medical officers. Between 4 January and 3 October 1879 there were 9,510 medical admissions from a military strength of 12,615. Of these admissions, 2,789 or 29.3 per cent were due to 'fever' whilst 1,522 or 16 per cent were due to enteric fever, dysentery and diarrhoea; there were 574 admissions from rheumatism. Any precise diagnosis under active service conditions was difficult and, according to the *HAMD:*

> There was much confusion over the separation of fevers due to different causes; this was overcome by an all-embracing diagnosis of 'typho-malarial' fever.

Janet's strong religious convictions made it difficult for her to reconcile the political motivation of some aspects of the war with her conscience, but she held her tongue and quietly went about her duty of tending the wounded and attempting to better the conditions of the common soldier. The treatment of wounds had not kept pace with the development of the means of inflicting them. True, chloroform now took away the terror of amputation while the victim was fully conscious but the chance of recovery was still horrifyingly low. Most amputees who died did so of shock and blood poisoning but, if a patient could survive the first few days, then he could be expected to live. This was exactly Janet's experience at Utrecht as, fortunately, her two doctors, Somerford and Fitzmaurice, were experienced and careful.

Conversely, most of the surgeons used by the Army did not enjoy such a good reputation and were regarded as little more than timeserving butchers, with the common nickname of 'sawbones' accurately bestowed upon their heads. There was generally a great shortage of doctors in the Army Medical Department and few wanted to serve in the Army. In 1868 there were 176 candidates for 100 vacancies, but in 1878 there were only forty-eight. The shortage was caused by the poor pay including poor sick pay, loss of a batman, few medals, honours or awards and low relative rank.

Curiously, another major cause for doctors leaving the Army Medical Department was the cessation of 'forage allowance'. Officers had a Royal Warrant to keep horses for their use, and a substantial allowance (the forage allowance) was paid. Doctors were officers; they did not require a horse, but received the allowance nonetheless. The withdrawal of this perk was a severe financial blow to many doctors and, in one fell swoop, the opportunities available to them in the colonies became very attractive. Consequently doctors of a poor quality were accepted into the Army Medical Department. Some, however, took their profession seriously and went to great lengths to learn from their experiences in the field. The two doctors Janet worked with at Utrecht were of the latter variety and she came to respect them and hold them in high regard. They, in turn, came to respect and admire her in her own professional capacity, and were more than happy to discuss the treatment of patients with her. They were highly impressed with her technical ability in treating the wounds of their patients as she was very skilful in handling the instruments and could debride a wound without causing any further trauma.

The majority of the soldiers' injuries that Janet faced were caused by either gunshot, assegai or throwing spear. The assegai had a short sharp broad blade and was used by the Zulu fighter as a forward stabbing weapon. The throwing spear was, as its name suggests, a long well-balanced spear for throwing. As long as the assegai or spear did not hit any vital organ, treatment of the wounds was very straightforward. Janet's standard practice was to cleanse the wound with Condy's fluid and then dress it with boracic lint or oiled silk and bandage it in place. Carbolic was only used to wash out dirty wounds. The Lister wound dressings that Janet had bemoaned the lack of in Vardin were found to be too bulky and impractical in the field in South Africa and were not used.

Gunshot wounds were a more serious matter as the bullet had to be removed to prevent blood poisoning. This was usually done by the surgeon using chloroform anaesthetic but Janet had, on occasions, to remove a bullet herself if no surgeon was available. These wounds were also cleaned with Condy's fluid or a zinc chloride solution and dressed with either boracic lint or oiled silk with a tenax outer dressing.

One particular surgeon, who kept meticulous and copious notes of his experiences in the field, was Surgeon D. Blair-Brown. His notes and observations and treatment of wounded solders and Zulus survive to this day. He used his service in South Africa to experiment with more effective ways of treating wounded men and to reject unsuccessful traditional methods and equipment. Extracts of his detailed and radical report found its way to the hospital at Utrecht and were avidly read by Janet and the surgeons there.

During the period of the Anglo Zulu War, as Sister Janet discovered at Utrecht, venereal disease turned out to be as large a threat to the British troops as the enemy, directly or indirectly causing more soldiers to seek medical assistance than any other ailment, although most of the severe cases were recorded as 'fevers'. For the troops, there was little or no official sex education and curiously, even the word 'syphilis' was banned from British newspapers until 1920. In June 1879, of the 300 cases being treated at the Durban military hospital, most patients suffered from malaria, dysentery or venereal disease. It can hardly be surprising that soldiers were syphilis's best friends. A soldier far from home, particularly one facing possible death from an assegai or from typhus, rarely bothered about sexual convention and accepted syphilis as the 'merry disease'. September 1879's *The Lancet* records that: 'Syphilis had been landed (at Cape Town and Durban) from the troopships, the disease having been contracted previously to the men leaving England.'

Syphilis apart, throughout the campaign the most ruthless killer of European mankind, one in six of all deaths, was tuberculosis, more commonly referred to as 'consumption', with about 60 per cent of the population suffering its long-term effects. Tuberculosis, or mycobacteriosis, is as old as humanity and the germ thrives when hosts, both humans and cattle, live in squalid and over-crowded conditions. It is spread by coughing and spitting, drinking contaminated milk and from contact with polluted water, grass, animal feed and soil. During the Anglo Zulu War, many soldiers joined the Army to escape the squalor and poverty at home, only to contract and then spread the disease wherever they lived in cramped and filthy conditions, and these were abundant during the Zulu campaign. It is unlikely that Army medical officers knew they were treating tuberculosis or even understood its cause. All too frequently during the campaign, soldiers were kept cramped together in extremely unhygienic conditions and within a week, previously healthy soldiers would succumb.

Following the battle at Rorke's Drift, some 600 soldiers slept for weeks in overcrowded conditions and squalor, others lived in equally unsanitary conditions during the siege at Eshowe, and at Fort Pearson similar cramped conditions resulted in mass sickness which was invariably attributed to the location and not the circumstances. Early stages of tuberculosis often produced no symptoms and soldiers could carry the disease for several years before they deteriorated. Symptoms common in the advanced stages of the disease included fever, fatigue, night sweats, loss of appetite, loss of weight, respiratory disturbances such as coughing, chest pains, and production of bloodstained sputum.

On campaign in Africa in 1879, the risk of death increased as the disease was invariably accompanied by viral or bacterial pneumonia, which was encouraged by cramped conditions or an absence of weatherproof accommodation. Common day-to-day illnesses and adverse conditions that constantly threatened the soldier in South Africa included severe sunburn, effectively treated by applying juice from the readily available aloe plant; diarrhoea, for which no treatment was available; rheumatism, no treatment until the sufferer was crippled; regular bouts of dehydration and heat exhaustion and blisters, for which the official treatment was 'threads of worsted to be drawn through the blister and the sock or garment, if available, to be well soaped over the injured part'.

The more serious medical cases that involved hospitalization included scarlet fever, measles, diphtheria, typhus, pneumonia, dysentery, polio and syphilis. The Army hospital at Gingindlovu recorded that in April they treated, out of seventy-six officers: fever one, sunstroke one, diarrhoea four, dysentery four, other diseases four. Out of 2,000 other ranks: fevers 180, rheumatism twenty-nine, diarrhoea forty, dysentery twenty-nine, bronchitis two, boils eleven; other diseases and accidental wounds forty-four. 'Other diseases' included venereal cases. The records reveal that the medical treatment for snakebite was copious alcohol (to be drunk). History records that the senior medical officer during the campaign, Surgeon General Woolfryes, blamed the atmosphere for the fevers and dysentery, while the soldiers knew little or nothing about protecting their food and water from the bacteria-carrying flies. Personal hygiene was still in its infancy, Colonel Clarke wrote: 'Latrines and urine pits were dug near the tents, and filled in every morning. The natives would not use them.'

Major MacGregor also lamented the natives' unfamiliarity with latrines and added: 'A principal difficulty was the constant death of oxen, often near water, which had to be dragged away and buried.'

A correspondent from the *Cape Argus* visiting Fort Tenedos on the Tugela River observed that it took three officers at a formally convened meeting to agree to replace a soldier's worn out boots while: 'Everyone ignored a dead ox lying in the stream immediately above the bathing place and water collection point.'

The sole attempt to purify the visibly contaminated drinking water was by the issue of charcoal filters to the troops but, although they were used, they had no effect against bacteria. There can hardly have been a time when there were so many frightening diseases and wounds for a young nurse to treat.

CHAPTER TWELVE

A one-sided interest

There was a legend in the area that the man who built the trading station at Rorke's Drift, which now bore his name, had a wife of great beauty. To visit Sarah Rorke and gaze into her eyes was the object of all gentleman hunters passing by or when returning from hunting trips to distant Mozambique. Other men, who attended James Rorke's funeral from Dundee and elsewhere, were collectively disappointed to see that the famous beauty was extraordinarily plain, if not downright ugly. After much discussion they unanimously came to the conclusion that the beauty perceived was purely due to her rarity value.

It was a very different story at the Army hospital at Utrecht; the presence of a pretty young English nurse caused a great deal of interest among the large number of young soldiers who had been starved of female company for many months. The sight of her walking from her house to the hospital ward each day caused a flurry of attention-seeking ploys between both the able bodied and her patients. At work, Janet became adept at sorting out the genuine calls for attention without hurting any male pride.

There was, though, one young admirer in particular who was a casualty in the hospital when Janet arrived at Utrecht. She soon noticed he spent much of his recuperation drawing sketches of Zulus, battle scenes and hospital life, in which Janet featured prominently. At first Janet found his attention amusing and regarded him in the same light as the majority of her patients.

111

Although nearly twenty years old, Janet had remained untouched by any romantic inclinations; she was a highly professional nurse and she knew that any relationship with a patient or colleague was strictly out of bounds.

T.H. (Harry) Peterson was a twenty-one year-old trooper in the colonial mounted volunteer regiment, the Frontier Light Horse. This unit had originally been commanded by Colonel Redvers Buller, who had moulded what had been a tough unruly bunch of mostly unemployed colonials into a disciplined and effective force. An example of how Buller dealt with even a mild case of rule infringement was illustrated by his handling of an unfortunate trooper who turned up on parade somewhat worse for drink. Pretending to ignore the matter, Buller led the unit out of camp on patrol. After several miles on the empty veld, he ordered the offender to dismount and left him to walk back to camp.

The Frontier Light Horse had made up part of the colonial volunteers who had been attached to Evelyn Wood's Column and had been highly active in raids upon Zulu villages and capturing cattle. During one badly planned raid on the mountain stronghold of Hlobane, the force of 600 horsemen came near to being completely wiped out when a large Zulu force trapped them on the flat hilltop. Harry Peterson was one who managed to scramble down the precipitous boulder-strewn slope called the Devil's Pass and, by fighting through the attacking Zulus, barely escaped with his life. He later sketched his recollection of this horrifying descent.

The following day, 29 March, Peterson's luck was put to the test again at the Battle of Khambula when the main Zulu army that had chased Buller's survivors away from Hlobane continued their advance with the intention of encircling Wood's column. It was thought the Zulus were on their way to destroy Utrecht and the other northern settlements, but in their path stood Evelyn Wood's well-prepared laager at Khambula Hill. Despite express instructions from King Cetshwayo not to attack any well-organized defensive position, the target was too tempting for the numerically superior Zulus, who included many warriors still flushed with success from Isandlwana and who deployed themselves into their familiar attacking formation of 'horns and chest'.

112

It was not long before the warriors began their intimidating and noisy ritual of striking spears against shields in preparation for a coordinated assault. Viewed from Wood's position, the Zulus made an impressive and frightening spectacle with their regiments distinguished by their different coloured cowhide shields. Once deployed, their advancing front covered nearly ten miles, an unnerving sight for the 2,000 British defenders. Wood decided to disrupt the Zulu's preparation for battle and ordered Buller to lead some thirty mounted colonial troops close to the Zulu front line to provoke their right horn into attacking prematurely.

Peterson was one of the group selected. They rode out towards the Ngobamakosi regiment standing a mile distant. Forming a line across their front, Buller's men reined in just 300 yards from the chanting warriors and dismounted, which for men who had barely escaped with their lives just twenty-four hours earlier, was a testing experience. Cocking their carbines, the volunteers fired a volley into the massed ranks, which had the effect of seriously agitating the impatient Zulu warriors. With a great shout of *uSuthu!* the Zulus surged forward in an uncontrolled charge. With the distance between the riders and the Zulus rapidly closing, the colonials mounted and rode for safety. Unfortunately, many of the horses were exhausted from the escape and long ride from Hlobane the previous day and the combination of the firing and the rapid approach of the yelling Zulus spooked some of them, making a number unmanageable. Two riders were overwhelmed and killed by the charging warriors.

Many of the Zulus had firearms and a shot from one of these hit Harry Peterson as he was about to mount his terrified horse. Major John Russell, a special service officer from the 12 Lancers, showed great bravery by dismounting and assisting the helpless Peterson into the saddle. Russell then found himself in difficulty as he was unable to steady his own horse. A black sergeant of the Natal Native Horse formed a screen around the officer to keep the Zulus at bay, while Lieutenant Edward Browne, of the Mounted Infantry, helped Russell onto his horse. In the nick of time, they were all able to turn and gallop back to the safety of the laager. For their bravery, Troop Sergeant Major Learda and

Lieutenant Browne were later awarded the Distinguished Conduct Medal and Victoria Cross respectively.

As for Major Russell, he received nothing; even his wish to be transferred to the remount depot in the safety of far-off Durban was not approved. Earlier in the year, in February, he had suffered a breakdown after witnessing the carnage and destruction of the camp at Isandlwana, which had badly affected his ability to lead his mounted command. Despite reluctance on both sides, Russell was sent to join Wood's Column and to serve under Redvers Buller. Having said that he would rather transfer to the remount depot than serve under Buller, Russell fell further from grace when, during the Hlobane debacle, he deliberately misinterpreted an ambiguously worded order from Wood and led his command away from the battle at a crucial moment. It was little wonder that Wood and Buller refused to put Russell's name forward for an award despite his undoubted, but belated, display of bravery.

For Trooper Peterson, in considerable pain at the crude field hospital and with the smoke and sounds of the battle for Khambula raging all around him, the war was over. Once the battle was won and the attacking Zulu army driven off, Peterson and the other fifty-six wounded were put into ox drawn wagons and slowly trundled along the twenty miles of rough tracks to the base hospital at Utrecht. Four weeks later he was well on the road to recovery when Sister Janet arrived.

Janet had read Peterson's notes and knew the circumstances of his injuries. His sketching was very therapeutic and Janet encouraged him to draw realistic scenes of the Zulus' domestic lives as well as battle scenes, which boded well for his psychological future as well as his physical recovery. As Harry recovered, his lively sense of humour returned and he spent hours composing rhymes and riddles to amuse the other rehabilitants on the ward; he also developed a one-sided interest in his nurse. Janet always kept a respectable distance between herself and her patients, including Harry Peterson, so that her professionalism was not compromised. Surgeon Major Fitzmaurice soon became aware of Trooper Peterson's growing interest in his pretty young nursing sister and, without discussing the subject with Janet, the clearly

114

lovesick young trooper was transferred to Durban to complete his recuperation.

The following day Sister Janet and Trooper Harry Peterson bade each other a mixed farewell. As she shook Harry's hand, he politely wished her well and sadly got into the cart for the long journey to Durban; he had already informed his friends that he would, somehow, find Sister Janet again one day.

CHAPTER THIRTEEN

Surrounded by death and sickness

Although Khambula has been acknowledged as the hardest fought battle of the Anglo Zulu War, and the one that turned the tide in favour of the British, the battle for Ulundi was the final act that effectively ended the conflict. Lord Chelmsford's second invasion of Zululand began on 31 May when his huge lumbering column crossed the Ncome River and re-entered Zululand. To the south, another massive column was advancing in a pincer movement to trap the still elusive remnants of the Zulu army. During the 100 mile march to the Zulu capital at Ulundi, which took a month to reach, Chelmsford heard that Wolseley had replaced him. Wolseley was hurrying from Durban by steamer to take up his new post but was thwarted by heavy seas when he tried to land on the beach at Port Durnford; his vessel had to return to Durban where Wolseley transferred to a horse-drawn cart and then faced a long cross-country journey of rutted tracks and numerous river crossings. Wolseley sent a telegram ordering Chelmsford to stop all operations, which was received on 2 July but Chelmsford's column was just four miles from Ulundi and poised to attack the Zulu capital.

In complete disobedience of Wolseley's order, Chelmsford formed an enormous square with his 5,000 troops on the plain within sight of King Cetshwayo's royal homestead. It was the morning of 4 July 1879. It took just thirty minutes for concentrated

116

British firepower to repulse the demoralized Zulu army before Chelmsford's mounted troops were released to pursue and slaughter the retreating warriors. King Cetshwayo had slipped away before the battle commenced and was now at large in the hills of Zululand. At long last, and to his great relief, Chelmsford's invasion of Zululand could now be officially declared a success and Wolseley had the good grace to offer his hearty congratulations. Chelmsford and his staff packed their bags and set off for Durban and the sea journey home. Chelmsford expected, and received, a hero's welcome on his return to England. There was little for Wolseley to do but instigate mopping-up operations and seek the capture of the elusive Zulu king. After six weeks of fruitless searching, King Cetshwayo's freedom was ended on 28 August and on 1 September the Zulu War was formally ended.

In a letter to his wife from his field headquarters at Ulundi, Wolseley described the capture and promised her, and the titled ladies on the Stafford House Ladies Committee, a small gift:

> I have managed to secure one of Cetshwayo's necklaces of lion's claws – only the highest in the land are allowed to wear such a distinction. I shall send to have a few of the claws to be mounted. You must write a note with each, saying I send a little 'charm', which formed part of Cetshwayo's necklace to Baroness Coutts, Lady Constance Stanley, Lady Sherbourne and Lady Cardwell.

Despite the one-sided nature of the battle for Ulundi, a large number of British participants were wounded, almost entirely from gunfire. Even the notoriously bad marksmanship of the Zulus could not fail to find targets amongst the massed ranks that formed the attacking British square. Now that the Zulus had been defeated, the British thirst for revenge after Isandlwana, which had coloured their attitude towards the Zulus, evaporated. A small number of wounded Zulus were collected from the battlefield and cared for by the victors. A few severely wounded Zulus were transported back to the base hospital at Utrecht along with seventy of the more seriously wounded British soldiers.

There had been considerable disquiet amongst the British public at the news that the Army had been slaughtering Zulu wounded in revenge for the way their own men had been killed and disembowelled at Isandlwana. It was reported that no wounded Zulu prisoners were taken or treated. This provoked Surgeon Major Cuffe, a recently arrived doctor at the Utrecht hospital, to write a letter which was printed in *The Times* on 9 September:

> In an answer to the statement recently made as to the non-reception of Zulu prisoners in hospitals, permit me to state as far as General Wood's column is concerned, wounded prisoners were frequently patients in the field hospital. The base hospital at Utrecht, a building hired by me with General Wood's sanction, for the treatment of natives, was constantly occupied by wounded Zulus and attended to by our staff. The prisoners themselves wondered at this kindness, and frequently told us that had our wounded fallen into their hands they would have assegaied them without mercy.

During Sister Janet's time at Utrecht there were many wounded Zulus among her patients and, once they overcame their initial fear that they were to be tortured, they came to revere her. They daily showed their gratitude by crawling to meet her as she approached their huts, kissing her dress and greeting her repeatedly. Janet had become used to natives from other tribes who worked at the hospital as orderlies, but she had only previously seen Zulu warriors at a distance. As patients, she had her first close encounter with them and she was amazed what remarkable specimens of manhood the Zulu warriors were compared with the average British soldier. Their black skins gleamed like oiled silk and the underlying rippling muscles reminded Janet of a racehorse in peak condition. She knew they were capable of running many miles and then fighting for hours with courage and ferocity, and without food or water. They did not appear to feel either the heat or cold being clad only in their loincloths, which seemed remarkably skimpy to the young nurse. The most

118

remarkable thing of all, Janet noted, was their feet. Used to running barefoot for mile upon mile over rocks, rough scrub and thorns, the skin on the soles of their feet was hard and horny, and as thick as the soles of a good pair of British Army boots.

A report confirming the nurses' role in caring for wounded Zulus appeared in the *Daily Telegraph* dated 3 October:

> The officers are not so well lodged as the men; but they are not by any means uncomfortable, and the work the sisters do in preparing drinks and tempting dishes, in watching and nursing, must be seen to be understood. There is a record of it in many a grateful look on the gentle faces of the devoted women who do their spiriting so tenderly.
>
> . . . two Zulu prisoners have been brought in here, and have been treated for their wounds. These men were as kindly treated and as well cared for as though they had been our own. One of these Zulus, Pashongo by name – a strange compound of gentleness and savagery – died a few days ago, and is still spoken of with the greatest regret in the hospital. He was badly wounded in the knee by a bullet at Ulundi and he quite won the hearts of those who attended him by his cheerfulness, patience and natural manner. The Stafford House nurse (Sister Janet) who attended him, writing to Surgeon-General Ross, observed that he had so gained the goodwill of the hospital orderlies that they would come twenty times a day to turn him and lift him up in their arms to give him ease. He was full of gratitude for the attention he received and every effort was made to save his life, but it was necessary to amputate the leg and the operation was followed by blood poisoning, of which he died.

Sister Janet commented in her report that the wounded Zulu was 'a better man than many a so-called Christian'. The *Telegraph* of 30 October reported General Wolseley's visit to Utrecht and again reported on the treatment of wounded Zulus:

> There was one outlying shed which escaped his notice; but in front of it, on the ground, in their blankets, were some

unfortunates whom he would have pitied, could he have seen them – six Zulu prisoners, wounded at the battle of Kambula (sic), who have been here ever since March. Hitherto, they have had a surgeon in attendance who spoke their language, but now they are under the charge of a kind-hearted orderly, who when I passed by, was trying to make them understand his meaning by a free use of pigeon English. They are all badly wounded, and three, at least, should have their legs amputated, but they will not submit to an operation, and the result is not doubtful.

Wolseley visited Utrecht on 11 September while en route from Ulundi to Pretoria. A special parade was assembled to which Sister Janet was specially invited. The *Natal Witness* reported:

At half past eight we had a parade of all the troops in the garrison, consisting of the 2-24th, three squadrons of Dragoons, and the detachment Royal Artillery with two guns, were drawn up in front of our head-quarters, in three sides of a square; and then the General attended by his Staff and many other officers rode onto the ground.

General Colley then called out for Brevet Major (Gonville) Bromhead and Private (Robert) Jones, who both came forward from the ranks; a letter from the Secretary of War to the General Commanding in South Africa was then read, and afterwards extracts from the *London Gazette*, giving the acts for which the Victoria Cross was to be presented.

Sir G. Wolseley having had the much-prized honours handed to him by Colonel Degacher said; 'Colonel Degacher and men of the 2-24th – the extracts just read describe very fully the two acts for which Her Majesty the Queen has been pleased to order these two crosses to be awarded. The Decoration is the highest one that a soldier can obtain, and it is naturally highly prized in consequence. It is worn at the present time by many brave officers and men in our army; but none better services to the State than those for which it

120

is given today, in gallantly defending Rorke's Drift against overwhelming numbers of savages; the defence, I believe, is only an instance of what British soldiers can do when properly handled and led. That fight will always be remembered with pride by every British regiment, as well as by the 2-24th; and when so thought of I feel sure the names of the two who now obtain the cross will be associated with it in the regimental annals, together with those other brave men who have also obtained the cross.

The General then pinned the crosses on their left breasts and wished them a long life and many opportunities of gaining other medals. The troops were then formed up and marched past, after which they were dismissed, and the General rode to see the laager and the town. Sister Janet later tried to engage Lieutenant Bromhead in conversation but, like so many before her, she found it difficult to illicit any response from him. Although not reported in the *Natal Witness* newspaper there was another recipient who received the Victoria Cross from General Wolseley at Utrecht that day. He was Private Samuel Wassall of the 80 Regiment who had been seconded to the Mounted Infantry. As the 80th were also stationed at Utrecht, prior to leaving the following day, it is probable that two consecutive parades were held, with the 24th Regiment following that of the 80th.

The *Daily Telegraph*'s correspondent then took up the story, no doubt to the delight of Sister Janet's family back in England. It reported:

> After the parade of Sept. 11, of the 24th Regiment, at which the Commander-in-Chief (Wolseley) affixed the Victoria Cross to the breasts of Major Bromhead and Private Jones for their share in the defence of Rorke's Drift, his Excellency visited the hospital, and made a minute examination of the condition of the patients, at the close of which, he expressed his satisfaction to the medical officers (Somerford and Fitzmaurice) in charge, and exchanged a few words with Sister Janet of the Stafford House Committee, whose care and attention to the sick are well worthy of notice, and have

been gratefully appreciated by those among whom she has been ministering.

Wolseley was not just being encouragingly polite when he praised Sister Janet, for she had become something of a local celebrity – particularly one so young and pretty – in a region conspicuously lacking in females. Her no-nonsense dedication coupled with her strong religious principles gained her much respect and there were no instances of her being propositioned or molested. Later, when Wolseley planned a campaign against the intransigent Swazi chief, Sekhukhune, an ongoing threat on the Transvaal frontier, he especially asked Sister Janet to travel to Standerton and accompany the expedition. In the event, wet weather intervened and the expedition was postponed until the end of the year.

Now that the fighting was over, orders came for the hospital at Utrecht to be dismantled and moved, by stages, to Durban via nearby Newcastle. The last of the wounded from Ulundi were taken to Newcastle although fifty sick, including four cases of typhus, had to remain until they were sufficiently recovered and well enough to travel. When the last of them was fit to depart, on 12 September, it was time for Sister Janet to leave. She was showered with thanks and the regret that she was leaving was obvious to all. The previously sceptical Surgeon Major Fitzmaurice wrote a glowing testimonial dated 13 September, in which he said:

I have great pleasure in testifying to the very excellent manner in which Sister Janet (Miss Wells), Stafford House Committee, has performed her duties at the Base Hospital at this station from July.

Miss Wells proved herself to be a thoroughly accomplished nurse; her attention to her duties and kindness to the sick and wounded under her care have been most praiseworthy, and she carries with her on leaving this station the gratitude of patients and staff alike.

Janet travelled with the sick to Newcastle. Her patients still required daily dressing of their wounds and many could not feed or wash themselves. She remained in Newcastle until she received an urgent message requesting her to travel to Landman's Drift on the Buffalo River. Wolseley's aide-de-camp, Lieutenant Henry John Hardy, had been taken sick with dysentery during the long first day's march from Ulundi on 3 September. Wolseley was forced to travel on to Utrecht and Pretoria without him but arranged for him to be brought to a field hospital at Conference Hill. Hardy remained there for three weeks, during which time there were constant storms and torrential rain. The flimsy hospital tent was scant protection and Hardy suffered from the cold and damp until it was decided to move the sick officer to a farmhouse near Landman's Drift. The change brought about an improvement in his condition and Sister Janet was summoned to attend him. Alas, she arrived just as Hardy had a relapse and died on 4 October.

Surrounded by death and sickness, Janet's life of hardship was not without its lighter moments. During the negotiations to persuade Sekhukhune to surrender, one of the conditions the intransigent Zulu chief insisted on was that he should be given a white wife. As Janet was the only white woman in the area, the rumour gained momentum that she was the chief's intended wife. For some time, she could not fathom why so many ordinary Zulu people lined her route to see her as she travelled through the towns and villages of the region. It became a standing joke amongst her colleagues and officers and she was thereafter named Mrs Sekhukhune.

CHAPTER FOURTEEN

To Rorke's Drift and Isandlwana

Sister Janet's work was not yet complete. Rorke's Drift was on her route back to Durban and because no doctor had visited the reduced British garrison for many weeks, she volunteered to visit the outpost, scene of the now famous battle. Once a suitable horse drawn cart could be found Janet set off on the sixty-five mile journey to Rorke's Drift. She considered taking a direct line south and then following the course of the Buffalo River to Rorke's Drift until she learned that no such route existed and worse, the area was uninhabited and would be unprotected by the Army. Janet changed her mind and agreed to make the longer journey via Dundee and Helpmekaar; it would be safer with other travellers occasionally using the marked route and accommodation could be found at both settlements. Having made her farewells, she retraced her journey to Dundee and on her arrival, her reputation having preceded her, she quickly found accommodation for the night and a fresh horse was made available for the onward journey to Helpmekaar.

By 6 a.m. the following morning Janet was ready to leave. The previous day had been uncomfortably hot and she wanted to make the most of the cool morning before the temperature rose. She was also entering new territory, which always excited her adventurous nature. Her track took her southwards out of the hamlet of Dundee and then climbed onto the top of the long ridge that formed the edge of the Biggarsberg plateau which follows the course of the Buffalo River. The route was uninspiring; long hill after long monotonous hill, except where, to the east, Janet was delighted with an occasional glimpse of the five-mile distant Buffalo River that formed the border between Natal and Zululand. Her journey took the best part of the day and she arrived at Helpmekaar during the mid afternoon. This former tiny hamlet was now a British Army supply depot and with the war over, its facility was no longer required by the Army and was in the process of being closed down. She was made very welcome and those present were, as ever, keen to accommodate her as an unexpected guest; all were hungry for any news she could bring.

Refreshed after a good night's sleep, she set off for the Rorke's Drift mission station. By now Janet was fully aware of the importance and growing fame of the outpost and her anticipation grew as her journey progressed. (See Appendix E for a brief account of the battle at Rorke's Drift.)

After only three miles from Helpmekaar, the track suddenly came to the edge of a precipice before winding its way down the steep rocky face. The guide was worried how to get his wagon safely down the twisting and steep track; both could clearly see the shattered remains of at least five Army wagons that had been lost before crashing onto the rocks below. There was no other route so, encouraged by Janet, they slowly and cautiously descended the 600 feet escarpment in a series of sharp hairpin bends. Where it was especially steep, the wagon driver placed rocks in front of the wheels to prevent the wagon running away from them while Janet held the horse's head and reins and made soothing noises.

After a nerve-racking hour they gained the safety of level ground. Janet was very relieved to have negotiated the precipitous bends, she now marvelled at the crystal clear views into Zululand. It was even possible to see the outline of Hlobane Mountain, some sixty miles away, where Trooper Peterson had been injured. Once on the level they made swift progress; the route was well-worn by the Army wagons and the thousands of troops who had marched along this very route in order to invade Zululand. Janet reflected that many had not made the return journey. Three hours later they arrived at the isolated mission station; the location was picturesque, sited on a rock outcrop under the lea of the Oskarsberg hill and facing the Buffalo River. The camp perimeter was guarded by two British soldiers who were astonished by the arrival of the young English nurse. They directed her to the nearby replacement Fort Melvill where Janet was introduced to the officer in charge of the rearguard, Lieutenant Rowden of the 99th Regiment. Following refreshments of tea and Army biscuits, he led her a short walk from the fort towards the river and her new accommodation. On receiving the news of her pending visit Lieutenant Rowden had thoughtfully arranged to have a Zulu hut constructed for her use; it was sited just a few hundred yards out of sight of the military accommodation.

This was to be her home for the next three weeks and Janet was delighted. The inside of the hut smelled pleasantly of freshly cut river reeds and inside and around the hut everything had been swept clean. Since entering Zululand she had been intrigued by Zulu huts and wrote that she was very surprised how comfortable these primitive buildings were. Zulu huts were designed to be cool in the intense summer heat and warm in winter and now she had her own hut, which thrilled her. The floor was of beaten earth and dung, now polished to a high shine; the woven windowless round wall rose to a point at the apex. As with all Zulu huts, hers had no opening, other than the open doorway, to release smoke from the wood cooking fire, sited on the central hearth, which ensured that the smoke-filled hut remained insect free. This wasn't a problem for Janet as she would take her meals at the nearby fort. A small fireplace had also been built next to her hut to supply hot water for her domestic use. A slatted bed and chair were her only comforts. She was so impressed by her new home, which she called 'our Mess hut', that she decided to paint the scene with the famous battleground of Rorke's Drift as the painting's backdrop. Perhaps she had been inspired to paint by Trooper Peterson because she eventually produced a remarkably accurate watercolour depicting her Zulu 'beehive' mess hut; in the picture, the battlefield of Rorke's Drift is clearly seen in the background. This rare and remarkable painting survives in her scrapbook.

She learned that the site of the famed defence had been abandoned due to its unsanitary condition hence the new Fort Melvill, which it replaced, overlooking the now famous Buffalo River crossing. The new fort was substantial, being built of dry wall construction; a deep ditch surrounded it with spiky aloes planted on the surrounding slopes. It had been named Fort Melvill, after Lieutenant Teignmouth Melvill, the adjutant of the 1/24 Regiment, who had ridden out of the massacred camp at Isandlwana with the Queen's Colour. With the war now over, the garrison had been reduced to a small rearguard that was in the process of preparing to re-join their regiment at Pinetown near Durban. The area was to be looked after by a retired trader, Mr Croft, until the eventual return of the Revd. Witt who was busy trying to make money in London suing the British government for the destruction of his house (unsuccessfully) and by lecturing on the battle (although he had not been present).

Soon Janet was busy and within a few days of arriving at Rorke's Drift she had managed to examine all the thirty-five British soldiers still stationed at the outpost. Most were in rude health, though the majority were suffering from abrasions and sores. The ubiquitous stomach problem that had bugged the whole invasion force from its outset was still the main medical problem. One of her first acts was to demand that the fort's daily drinking water was collected upstream from the river and then boiled. Under her direction, the camp's cooking utensils and cutlery were sterilized by boiling after each meal and within days the men's health improved. A laundry was also set up to wash the soldiers' bed linen, underclothing and shirts. Eight sick men suffering from 'fever' were confined to two tents outside the small fort so as not to spread infection further. As she fully expected, her arrival had a noticeable effect on the men that included a daily queue of curious soldiers suddenly possessed of a variety of complaints that included septic blisters, and in-comprehensible 'headaches and sprains'. The young nurse's no nonsense approach was noticeably effective as, within days, she managed to get most of the sick men on their feet and fit enough to resume their duties. The sight of the pretty young English nurse flitting between her hut and the fort worked wonders for the men's morale. Even the two remaining fever cases responded well to her treatment and both were soon able to eat solid food and gain their feet. Janet also demanded a complete tidy up of the fort area and all litter was burned.

She now had a little more leisure time and indulged herself with a touch of feminine vanity. She was able to wash her hair using a little of the green enema soap, a marvellous shampoo as many generations of nurses will testify. This was rinsed off using an infusion of locally collected herbs, in which her recently washed uniforms were also rinsed.

With the fort now less of a health hazard and with the men taking a modicum of pride in their appearance, Janet turned her attention to the immediate area around the fort. The war was now over and the local Zulu people, like those at Utrecht, were reputed to be non-threatening. She was fully aware of the battles that had recently taken place at Rorke's Drift and nearby Isandlwana, and with the health of the small garrison under control, she requested an escort to visit the nearby battle locations. During her first day at Rorke's Drift she had been shown over the battlefield by Lieutenant Rowden who had pointed out the notable locations to her. She was especially interested in the ruin that had been Surgeon Reynolds's makeshift hospital and both fell silent before the neat row of graves at the rear of the building. The pair then walked the 100 yards to the site of James Rorke's grave. Janet knew that James and his wife had founded the small but modern habitation when the Rorke family settled at the Drift as traders in 1849. James shot himself in 1875 after his supply of gin ran out, leaving his wife destitute. His will demanded his being buried under solid concrete one yard deep to prevent the Zulus exhuming his body for use in their manufacture of *muti* or medicine. James Rorke knew only too well that body parts of well-known and respected white people were in great demand by the Zulus for *muti*.

Janet began to collect souvenirs of her time in South Africa. There seemed to be an endless supply of Zulu weapons and shields available around the camp and she gathered a small collection. Like many young Victorian women her interest was not militaria; she picked and pressed local flowers, ferns and grasses into an impressive album that survives to this day.

Janet had eagerly accepted the opportunity to meet a local *Sangoma* or medicine man. She had come across a number of local herbal remedies during her time at Utrecht, remedies which she knew worked very well. She was also particularly interested in the Zulu treatment of wounds. She remembered Dr Blair-Brown's report of a Zulu warrior who had a gunshot wound to his leg, which was successfully treated with the leaf of an orchid commonly found on the veld. The *Sangoma* told Janet of many other remedies to be found growing nearby and presented her with a skin bag containing herbs; she recorded their purpose as being 'fertility enhancing'. He was, however, reticent about discussing the snuff the warriors took before battle, which Janet knew was a mind-influencing drug used to stir the fighters to greater ferocity. To divert her attention he performed an amazing display of incantations and dances which exhorted the spirits to act on behalf of the warriors.

Janet was also taken for an hour's ride on horseback to the top of the Oskarsberg, the hill which dominated the fort and river crossing, from where she marvelled at the panorama of the Buffalo River far below. Across the valley she could see Isandlwana mountain just ten miles to the east. Her guide then took her down the far side of the Oskarsberg; she was pleased to be guided through the mass of boulders to join the old wagon trail that led from Rorke's Drift to Sotondose's Drift, recently renamed Fugitives' Drift, where the few Isandlwana survivors crossed back into Natal. It had been the only point where the survivors could attempt to cross the river in their flight from the battle. The purpose behind her guide's detour was to show Janet the caves and bushmen's paintings on the east side of the Oskarsberg, which had been discovered by the fort's soldiers a few weeks earlier.

The paintings had been drawn in prehistoric times, which indicated how long the area had been settled. Janet was fascinated by the skilful drawings and the vivid colours of the animals portrayed, which included deer, buffalo, lion and elephant, mostly being hunted by the dwarf-like figures of the bushmen. Her guide then took her to the bank of the Buffalo River and, by hitching up her long skirt, she was able to wade across the fast-flowing river to the far bank. The site of her crossing was, of course, the very point which gave the location its name, the only point for twenty or so miles in each direction where the river runs across an outcrop of submerged rocks. On the far side she was taken to see the neat and recently constructed second British cemetery just 100 yards from the river. The cemetery was the final resting place of those soldiers who had died of fever during the invasion of Zululand and who, according to the wisdom of the time, had to be buried well away from the fort itself.

The following day, a horse was found for Janet and she was taken to Fugitives' Drift, about six miles from Rorke's Drift, where Lieutenants Melvill and Coghill were buried in rough graves high on the steep slope above the now gently flowing Buffalo River. Even though it was just a few months since their deaths, there was already a romantic legend that was becoming accepted as fact. This was soon reinforced when several paintings and engravings were presented to the public by the leading British newspapers of the day, for the Victorians loved dead romantic heroes. (See Appendix D for the full account.)

During Janet's stay at Rorke's Drift she was asked to go to the nearby homestead of a local Zulu chief in an endeavour to help some of the village children who were suffering with eye infections. Having strapped her medical kit to her horse she was escorted some five miles beyond the river to the homestead of Chief Sihayo, which had been attacked by the British force following the invasion of Zululand earlier in the year. On arriving at the homestead, the Zulus were surprised to see Janet, in her nurse's uniform, on horseback and with only two riders as escort. She was taken to Chief Sihayo who, following the usual protracted ritual of a Zulu greeting, clapped his hands loudly; the afflicted children, who had been peering from behind a row of huts, reluctantly came forward. Janet noted that very few had any semblance of clothing. During the next two hours she treated them by bathing their eyes with a boracic solution and instructed the Zulu mothers how to bathe their children's eyes properly without constantly re-infecting them. After she had finished her ministrations and had duly handed out sugar pieces to the children, Sihayo invited his guests to watch a display of dancing by some of his men. The warriors were a spectacular sight in their full war dress of loin covering pelts, ankle and wrist bracelets woven from animal hair and headdresses of animal skin bands with feathers. They carried purposeful looking hide shields and spears.

The dance was a depiction of a battle which showed the head of the buffalo leading the attack followed by the chest and horns formations then coming in to surround and overwhelm the enemy. There was a great deal of foot stamping and kicking of legs in the air, and banging of spears on shields. The men were accompanied by drums of different sizes and singing from the rest of the village. As the men passed Janet by, throwing their legs into the air, she observed that there was nothing being worn under the skimpy loincloths. The dance of the maidens followed; a band of unmarried Zulu girls commenced to dance, all with eyes downcast, each girl holding a stick to represent a dagger. They wore short grass skirts and bracelets of beads woven into intricate designs. The girls were naked from the waist up and a startled Janet had never seen so many bare breasted women in all her life. The chief explained as best he could that the dance was to exhibit the girls' assets to potential husbands. Most of the male dancers were mature men as the price of a bride was too high for the young warriors. Janet recalled seeing several men with recent wounds and noted that there was no sign of any infection. It was clear from their shy demeanour that they were reluctant to allow her to approach them; she respected their attitude by concentrating her attention on the children.

Later that afternoon Janet returned with her guide to Rorke's Drift. It was nearly sunset when, alone, she walked round the burned out abandoned hospital where those brave defenders had died trying to protect their sick and wounded comrades. She stood outside the remains of the store where Surgeon Reynolds had continued to operate under the onslaught of the Zulu attacks. The remnants of the defensive position were still evident and she wondered at the small size of the area where a few brave men defended the hospital building against the powerful and well-armed Zulu force sent to destroy them. She was now especially glad that she had been present at the parade when Sir Garnet

131

Wolseley had presented Major Bromhead with his Victoria Cross. Following the presentation at Utrecht, she had briefly tried to speak with the new Victoria Cross recipient and later noted that she had not been very impressed with the partially deaf, inarticulate Major, but standing here at the scene of his triumph she felt ashamed of her earlier disdain. The glowing evening sun set very quickly and soon the site was in shadow. The cool of the evening sent her hurrying down to the warmth and light of her mess hut and her evening meal.

At dawn two days later, accompanied by an escort rider and a guide, Janet left Rorke's Drift to ride to the Isandlwana battlefield. She had often heard of the defeat by the Zulu army of Lord Chelmsford's Army and, like many visitors then and now, she was curious to visit the site of the disaster. The small group travelled lightly with just one packhorse carrying her tent and cooking utensils; they planned to be away from Rorke's Drift for two days. The route along the track was easy to follow, the open countryside was marked by the rutted tracks of the hundreds of wagons that had accompanied the ill-fated invasion. The marsh area that had so hindered Chelmsford's column back in January was now completely dry and the rivers were little more than streams and were easy to ford. After a steady two hour ride under the lea of the Nqutu hills, they reached the battlefield. They breakfasted on the gentle rise of land between the Isandlwana hill and Black's Koppie. From their picnic spot they had a clear view of the ten miles back to Rorke's Drift and, in the other direction, they could see over the whole devastated campsite area.

Beyond the obvious cairns that marked the graves, they could see for some fifteen miles along the uninhabited three-mile wide grassy valley towards the waterfall at the Mangeni homestead that lay in the direction of Ulundi. The camp area presented a forlorn and woeful sight. All the 1,400 bodies on the British side had only recently been buried under some 300 large stone cairns, some ten feet high, but the ground was still scattered with the whitening bones of slain horses and oxen. Her guide pointed out the main features of the battlefield and Janet then set off, alone, to walk round the remains of the campsite. During the next hour she came across a variety of relics including pieces of wood and metal that had clearly belonged to pieces of military equipment, muddled up with Zulu spearheads and sticks. There were tent pegs, cartridge cases, broken glass, meat and sardine tins, horse bones and, to her horror, the occasional half-buried skeleton. Janet noticed that there were pieces of paper that had been caught in bushes or which lay among the rock outcrops that littered the area. She collected a number of these papers as souvenirs, some of which seemed so poignant such as a frontispiece from Dickens's *Pickwick Papers*, complete with Boz's drawing of Pickwick meeting Sam Weller and part of a letter signed '*From your own Madgie'* and still legible despite being exposed to sun and rain for nearly ten months. She also picked up two pages of Romans and Corinthians torn from a pocket bible. She found a page ripped from a soldier's pay book which had belonged to Private Thomas Vedler of C Company, 2/24 Regiment, who had perished along with Captain Younghusband and all his comrades as they made a valiant last stand on the slope of the mountain. Lack of ammunition forced them into making a hopeless bayonet charge into the mass of Zulus in the forlorn hope they could fight their way out of their predicament.

Janet later recalled that amidst the scene of battle there were isolated clumps of grasses and small bright spring flowers and she collected the prettiest for her scrapbook and diary. Everywhere she walked there was evidence of where soldiers had stood and fought to the death. Piles of bright brass cartridge cases were glinting in the sun; one of these she added to her growing collection of artefacts.

After picking their way through the natural jumble of rocks that were a feature of the area, the party then rode up onto the Nqutu Ridge that overlooks the whole Isandlwana plain. From her viewing point, where King Cetshwayo's generals had exhorted their regiments into battle, she had a clear overview of the wrecked British campsite that had been so unsuspecting beneath the strangely shaped peak of Isandlwana mountain. Janet felt the haunting sadness of the place where so many young men had died such hideous deaths; the scattered stone cairns every few yards forming a collective monument to the British Army's catastrophic loss.

By mid-morning she was ready to continue the ride for a further ten miles to Mangeni Falls where Lord Chelmsford had taken lunch while, unbeknown to him, his camp was being destroyed. She recalled that, like the day of the battle, the day was hot and she was keen to see the waterfall of which so many at Rorke's Drift had spoken. She was not to be disappointed. The group had an easy ride along the well-worn traders' track that ran parallel with the nearby Malakatha hills and easily reached the falls by mid-afternoon. Janet was startled when she first saw that a small stream they were following led them to the head of an unexpected deep gorge where the water cascaded 600 feet vertically downwards to the beautiful deep blue lake at the bottom. She was astonished by the size of the waterfall and gingerly inched forward to the very edge to look over the steep drop. She spent some time watching the gull-like birds swooping after flies before returning to their nests that littered the steep cliff face.

The group then rode on for a further half-mile round the rim of the gorge where they intended to stop for the night. Her two escorting soldiers produced a small bivouac tent for Janet and set about making a comfortable campsite. Janet, ever inquisitive, climbed down onto a narrow terrace of rocks overlooking the waterfall and sat on a precarious rock overlooking the chasm to admire the view, now bathed a deep red by the setting sun. It was only later during their evening meal that she learned that this was the very same spot where Lord Chelmsford had lunched on 22 January, and where he had received the news that his force at Isandlwana had been overwhelmed. During their meal, illuminated by a candle lamp, a number of Zulu children crept up to their campsite and peered at the visitors through the grass. Janet's attempts to encourage the children to come forward all failed as no doubt the children had listened to their parents' understandable warnings not to get too close to white people.

Janet wrote that the nights in Zululand were frequently cold and that night at Mangeni was no exception. The following morning she was pleased to get going and they were well on their way by 8 a.m. The next location on her route was the Ngwebeni Valley that lay hidden from the British camp at Isandlwana and which had been the secret assembly point for the Zulu army before it attacked the unsuspecting British position. No one knew how the Zulu army had managed to get 30,000 warriors accompanied by 5,000 Zulu women and youths to within four miles of the British camp without the British scouts being aware of their presence. Janet thought it was a tall story and wanted to see the location for herself.

The fifteen mile route from Mangeni took them through a series of low rocky hills along a well-worn Zulu track. They passed a handful of Zulu homesteads and, apart from the ubiquitous inquisitive children, Janet saw few adults. They reached the Ngwebeni Valley at midday and Janet recalled that she was surprised to ride up a gently inclined rocky hillside and then, at the top, find that it dropped sharply away for several hundred feet to a beautiful river valley far below. It was certainly a very secret place and totally unseen from Isandlwana. She was intrigued by the meandering river beneath her and immediately requested to ride down to it. The journey down, over tightly packed boulders, took another half an hour. At the bottom it became just another river in Zululand with water running over rocks and boulders and small children seeming to appear from nowhere to view the visitors.

One thing did, however, catch her attention: piles of empty and abandoned British cartridge cases were strewn along the riverbank. She later learned that the returning Zulu army paused at Mangeni where the Zulus rested for the night following the battle. The following day, many hours had been spent pulling the bullets from the cartridges and then pouring the powder into Zulu powder horns for subsequent use in their antiquated but cherished muskets. Janet's group then followed the river upstream towards the ridge that led onto the grassy plateau overlooking Isandlwana. The group stayed on the high ground until they could see Rorke's Drift in the distance. It was then just a steady ride back to camp which they reached at dusk. Janet later estimated that she had ridden eighty miles in two days. She was pleased with her collection of wild flowers and she spent the next day carefully pressing the flowers between sheets of paper.

A few days later news reached the small Rorke's Drift garrison that they were to abandon the fort and join their regiment at nearby Dundee, prior to marching back to Durban. Janet was ordered to report to Durban directly where she would embark for passage back to England. But Durban was some 200 miles distant and she knew the journey would take another week. She was allocated a local guide, who claimed to know the way and who would drive her cart, and one soldier escort. On 17 October she bade the few remaining soldiers farewell and set off back along the well-worn traders' track to Helpmekaar where they would join the main dirt road to the small Walton family homestead further south on the Tugela River which, in turn, would lead her in the direction of the European village at Greytown.

The journey was one of endless green hills and rocky river crossings and each day her small party made steady progress. From Greytown the rough dirt roadway was in better condition and they trotted along at a good speed. They reached Pietermaritzburg on 20 October where, to Janet's relief, she was accommodated at one of the new hotels. It was the first occasion that she could enjoy the pleasure of a hot bath since leaving Utrecht three weeks earlier. Her clothes were washed and she managed to trim her unruly fringe, which had grown too long. The following day her small party resumed their journey to Durban where she arrived on the evening of 22 October 1879. As she descended off the inland plateau of hills towards Durban she felt the oppressiveness of the rising heat and humidity that envelopes the Indian Ocean coastline; hot and bothered, she arrived at the port and reported to the embarkation office. To her relief she was directed to a nearby hotel and accommodated in some luxury until her vessel, the *Dublin Castle*, was due to depart a few days later.

Sister Janet could now return home in the knowledge that her mission had been a complete success. She was excited about the prospect of her journey, especially as the boat, the same *Dublin Castle* that took her to Africa, would be stopping en route at Cape Town to enable the Stafford House team to reunite for the long sea voyage home.

When the boat stopped at Cape Town on 2 November, there was sufficient time for Janet to be received by King Cetshwayo, who was being held a prisoner at the castle prior to being sent to

136

England to meet with Queen Victoria. The Zulu king had become something of a tourist attraction for officers returning home and he rather enjoyed the respectful attention he received. Janet was very surprised by King Cetshwayo. He had already heard of her kind treatment of Zulu warriors at Utrecht and was pleased to meet her. Talking to Captain Ruscombe Poole, the officer commanding his guard, she learned something of his lifestyle. The King was a grossly obese man with a large belly who took very little exercise, his royal authority being based on strategy and diplomacy. He was still an imposing looking man and in his youth he had been a remarkable athlete and an outstanding warrior. His diet, in view of his regal position, was mainly meat. He had numerous wives who visited him at his command. His first wife, however, stayed at his side most of the time. Janet, like a true Victorian maiden, drew a veil over the King's, to her mind unconventional, domestic arrangements. When Janet met him he was clearly suffering from an uncomfortable stomach complaint and, through his interpreter, Henry Longcast, the young nurse proposed a solution and was duly given permission to relieve the King.

The combination of a diet with little fruit and fibre and a lack of exercise were not conducive to a good digestive transit. Without further ado, and knowing exactly what to do, Janet collected some enema soap, rubber tubing, funnel and a bucket, and after mixing a large hot mixture of soap and water soon relieved the King of his discomfort. With the mission accomplished, she left him with a large bottle of castor oil to ensure the royal colon did not get blocked again. As a mark of gratitude for this, and in recognition of Janet's work with the wounded Zulus at Utrecht, King Cetshwayo presented her with his matching necklaces and bracelets, which survive to this day.

The Stafford House team were the last of the nurses to leave South Africa as they were obliged to wait for both Chief Commissioner Ross and Dr Stoker, who had been closing the accounts of the committee at their nurses' respective locations. It was later estimated that as many as 3,200 sick and wounded soldiers passed through Sister Janet's hands at Utrecht, ranging from the seriously sick and wounded to those suffering from minor complaints like sunburn and blisters. For Sister Janet, the South African experience had been rewarding and one that contrasted with her harrowing service in Bulgaria. She had been supervised by a kindly and efficient gentleman in Chief Commissioner Surgeon General Ross and gained the respect of the two Army doctors at Utrecht. Her patients had been grateful and some, like Harry Peterson, had become seriously devoted. Janet had loved South Africa, particularly the beauty of the wide open veld of Zululand.

On 3 November 1879 the Stafford House party was reunited on board the *Dublin Castle*, which sailed from South Africa for home the following day. Sister Janet's nickname, Mrs Sekhukhune, spread rapidly around the ship, which, combined with the tales and rumours of her exploits in Zululand, only enhanced her popularity with her fellow travellers. She later recalled how excited she became as the vessel entered the English Channel. This was to be her second homecoming from a major military campaign. She had returned home from the Balkans two years earlier, exhausted and undernourished but this time she was returning home suntanned, brimming with health and full of enthusiasm to tell exciting stories to her awaiting family. She was also looking forward to her twentieth birthday.

Official appreciation for the services of the Stafford House nurses, however, was mixed. In his report to the War Office, the Surgeon General of Natal, J.A. Woolfryes, wrote:

The Sisters of Charity belonging to the Convent at P.M. Burg having rendered their services, 3 of them were employed at an early period of the war at Fort Napier Base Hospital. In March an application having been made to the Bishop of Bloemfontein, the Lady Superior & 3 Sisters of the Community of St Michael & All Angels were sent to Ladysmith and did good work in the Base Hospital there.

Towards the close of June, 2 Lady Sisters of the All Saints at Cape Town, who had gained experience in the Franco-German war, were despatched to Durban with a trained nurse by Lady Frere, and performed excellent service in the Base Hospital at that station, being transferred to the

Convalescents Depot at Pinetown on the arrival of Lady Superintendent Deeble and 6 nurses, and Surgeon General Ross, C.I.E, with 7 sisters of the Stafford House Committee in July. Of the Netley nurses, 4 with Mrs Deeble were posted to Durban and the remaining 2 to Newcastle. Of the Stafford House sisters, 4 remained at Durban, 2 were sent to P.M. Burg and 1 to Utrecht but this institution was subsequently modified according to circumstances.

Surgeon General Woolfryes then delivered a deliberately worded snub to the civilian Stafford House team:

All the nurses, but most especially those belonging to Netley, under the able superintendence of Mrs Deeble, and of the religious communities did much excellent work and contributed very materially by their tender care and skilful nursing to alleviate the suffering of the sick and wounded. I might add that by their example they stimulated the Hospital Orderlies to greater earnestness and zeal in the performance of their duties.

By singling out the Army's own nurses and the local religious orders for praise, Woolfryes was able to diminish the role played by the civilian Stafford House medical team. Still smarting from Wolseley's criticism of senior medical officers and his insistence in sending the Stafford House House medical team to help, Woolfryes blatantly attempted to get his own back. The Army establishment ungallantly sought to withhold due recognition of the service rendered by Sister Janet and her colleagues by delaying the issue of their South Africa Campaign Medals. Mrs Deeble and her six nurses received their medals on 19 October 1880, while the Stafford House nurses and doctors had to wait nearly four years until 15 July 1884 before receiving theirs.

Surgeon General Ross was, however, enthused by the Stafford House nurses. He wrote:

I believe that while all the medical officers fully recognize the value of the Sisters in their nursing capacity, they also felt

139

their presence a great aid in maintaining regularity in the hospitals. The respect in which the Sisters were held both by patients and orderlies was very noticeable; and I would add, that the more refined the lady the more her influence was felt.

I consider the employment of trained Sisters is a great instrument in aiding the preservation of regularity and good order in military hospitals.

In contrast to the Army's mealy-mouthed attitude, the local population, as represented by the Archdeacon of Natal, delivered a glowing testimonial dated 28 October 1879:

To Surgeon-General Ross, C.I.E, and the Ladies of Stafford House Committee who leave Natal this day for England. Much respected Christian Friends, – Were you permitted to quit these shores after all the kindness shown by each and all of you to the many wants of our brave soldiers, who have done so great service to their country by protecting the white inhabitants of South Eastern Africa from the invasion of their enemies, I may, I think, venture to say that the people of this Colony would, in this instance, be guilty of an omission which, to them, would be a cause of much regret.

May I then be permitted, as Acting Military Chaplain, to offer you all our warmest expressions of gratitude for the unvaried attention and kindness which, during your stay in Natal, have been shown to the sick and wounded, to whom your watchful care has been so tenderly extended, and by whom it has been so fully appreciated.

To the Ladies and Gentlemen composing the Stafford House Committee the Colonists need hardly say that no words of theirs can adequately convey their sense of the value of so noble an effort as that in which they are engaged in administering with so much generosity to the relief of suffering humanity.

May God's blessing continue to direct and prosper its most benevolent designs in the earnest prayer of those who have received so great a proof of their Christian sympathy.

I, on behalf of the Colonists at large, beg to thank the

Committee and yourselves with all our hearts, and to subscribe ourselves,

Your very grateful servants,

W.H.C. Lloyd, Archdeacon of Natal and his fellow-countrymen

Sister Janet and her Stafford House Committee had treated many thousands of serving soldiers under difficult circumstances who would certainly have endorsed this glowing testimonial. (See Appendix F for details of press reports relating to Sister Janet.)

The overall cost of sending the Stafford House team to South Africa amounted to £5,034, which was divided into the following percentages of the total:

Travel by sea	1.40
Travel by land	12.06
Board and lodging	4.76
Post	.12
Telegraph	.34
Banking	1.86
Sisters' salaries	3.84
Sisters' purchases	1.4
Cost of hospitals	73.74
Miscellaneous	.48
Total:	100 per cent

Expenses of Stafford House team in South Africa

Expended in:	£	Days under supply	Patients sick	Daily
Base hospital Durban	2,607	103	23,736	230
Base hospital Pietermaritzburg	464	82	8,517	103
Field hospital Ladismith (sic)	306	142	11,652	84
Field hospital Newcastle	142	156	6,745	43
Field hospital Utrecht	83	52	3,201	62

Cork leg for Gunner Burslem £14-5s-0d

The total expenditure for the supply of comforts, necessities etc. to the hospitals was £3,687. The sums made over to the medical officers were often usefully expended in repairs or sanitary additions. Overall, the Stafford House nurses conducted a total of 53,851 medical administrations, the average cost per patient being 1s 4d although for officers it rose to just over £2.

CHAPTER FIFTEEN

Home at last

The long sea journey home to England was relaxed and for
Sister Janet, a most enjoyable experience. Although eager
to see her family again and determined to resume her
nursing duties at the Tottenham Hospital, Janet spent many
happy hours with her fellow nurses on board comparing notes on
their experiences. Sister Emma Durham, the comic in the party
who had been assigned to Ladysmith, frequently caused great
mirth with her repeated account of the arrival of Mrs Deeble with
her Netley group of nurses and of their soaking in the storm.
Emma was a great raconteur, mimicking the portly Mrs Deeble
leading her 'gels' out to the tents, having declined the accommodation that Emma had provided for them and then, like a mother
hen, leading the bedraggled and wide-eyed group back from
their storm battered and collapsed tents.

On arriving at Dartmouth, the Stafford House team caught the
train to London and all went their respective ways to various
parts of the capital. Janet enjoyed an emotional family reunion at
Waterloo station and her apprehensive family was greatly
relieved to find her in such good health. After her long months
away, she was given leave to be with her family and friends and
it was during this interlude that she attended a London concert
given by the Stafford House Committee in honour of the newly
returned medical team from South Africa. Benjamin Wells was
the guest artist playing the Mozart flute concerto and Janet
was one of the guests of honour. George King was also a guest;

handsome and personable as well as being a noted and popular journalist with a shrewd eye for business, he had written for the *Illustrated London News* before becoming its advertising manager. Instantly attracted to the pretty nurse, he made it his business to effect an immediate introduction. Janet had long been accustomed to soldiers surreptitiously staring at her and now that she was something of a celebrity, such attention was the norm. The following day George left his calling card at the Wells' home and his persistence was rewarded when Janet agreed to 'walk out' with her enthusiastic suitor. It was not long before the two fell in love. Janet now realized the difference between a passing romantic episode and the growing love she felt for George King. Their courtship followed the gentle pattern of most middle class Victorian couples. Walks in the park together, visits to family and friends, trips to the theatre and, of course, the many concerts given by her father and sisters and brother. The only difference was Janet's work at the Tottenham Hospital. Janet duly notified Dr Laseron of her engagement and, delighting in her happiness, he readily gave his consent for George to collect her from the hospital in his hansom cab in order to escort her to church and to visit her parents.

At about this time, having recovered from his wounds and with the money for a ticket now in his pocket, Harry Peterson booked his passage to England to seek out Sister Janet. Although Harry's journey had been unknown to Janet, on his arrival in London she agreed to see him. Little is known of their meeting other than a brief diary note confirming that Harry presented Janet with his folio of drawings. He learned of her engagement and with any romantic aspirations now dashed, Harry Peterson returned to South Africa. Nothing more was heard of him but all his sketches survive in Janet's collection, including a self-portrait of a mounted bugler in the throes of dramatically being thrown from his horse during the retreat from Hlobane. This was clearly traced from an engraving entitled *The Last Call* that appeared in the June edition of the *Illustrated London News* depicting a statuette being then exhibited at the Royal Academy. Another sketch he entitled *Ministering Angel* shows Sister Janet carrying a basket of comforts and handing a jar of plum jam to a heavily bandaged patient. A further drawing gave a wider depiction of the interior of a hospital hut with the wounded, many of whom were amputees, shown lying on pallets raised barely six inches from the floor. The hastily constructed wooden walls were adorned with framed pictures and an Army bell tent is visible through the open door. Naturally, Peterson featured in most of the drawings.

On 6 May 1882, at Shepherd's Bush, Janet Wells became Mrs George King. She had earlier received Dr Laseron's blessing to leave the Deaconesses in order to become a full-time wife to her ambitious husband. Her association with nursing was not entirely severed for she kept abreast of nursing developments and contributed to various debates on the role of women in nursing casualties of war. She believed passionately that women had a big role to play in the treatment and care of the wounded and sick on the battlefield.

The Times reported the marriage and alluded to the possibility of her wartime experiences being published; sadly this would not occur until 123 years later. *The Times* report said:

> For her devotion and care she was complimented by Sir Garnet Wolseley and highly reported by Surgeon General Ross. Doubtless, our readers will be glad to hear that Miss Wells – now Mrs George King – intends to publish a history of her work and adventures. This volume may well be expected to be intensely interesting, for, so far as we know, no writer has yet written on the aspect of these wars as seen by one whose work was to save, and not to destroy, life.

The following year, she received the profession's highest accolade. Queen Victoria, a great believer in rewarding merit with an impressive medal, instituted her own recognition of ladies who had given exceptional service in the field of military nursing. The Royal Red Cross was a handsome decoration consisting of a red enamelled gold cross containing on each of the four arms, Faith, Hope, Charity and 1883, with Victoria's effigy in the centre and the Royal Cipher in the reverse centre. The Cross was suspended from a red and blue bow.

The notification of the award arrived by post from the War

Office dated 24 August 1883. The covering letter was brief and to the point:

> The Queen commands the decoration of the Royal Red Cross, which Her Majesty has been pleased to confer upon you for the special devotion and competency which you have displayed in your nursing duties with Her Majesty's Troops.

Other recipients included the royal princesses, who were patrons of various voluntary aid organizations. The first nurse recipient was, naturally, Florence Nightingale, who was obliged to decline receiving her award personally from the Queen as she had become virtually housebound. The second group of recipients were the Stafford House nurses who saw service in South Africa; Sisters Edith Horner, Emma Durham and Edith King, were also rewarded, as well as the now heavily pregnant Sister Janet. Mrs Deeble and several of her Netley staff who had served in Zululand, Transvaal and Egypt were also granted the award.

Janet was both highly honoured and delighted to receive the Royal Red Cross decoration, which complemented the South Africa Medal she had recently received. Within two weeks of giving birth to her first daughter, Elsie, her husband arranged for her to be photographed in her Red Cross uniform wearing the Royal Red Cross decoration and her South Africa Medal.

In the March 1885 edition of the popular *Illustrated Naval and Military Magazine*, an article appeared, written by Captain Charles Burgess, one of the pioneers of the British Red Cross, detailing Sister Janet's exploits and reporting on her receipt of the Royal Red Cross. (see Appendix A)

Any stated ambition she had of writing her life story seems to have been permanently shelved by motherhood. After a gap of ten years, the Kings had another daughter whom they named Daisy. Both daughters inherited the Wells's talent for music with Elsie becoming a regular performer at the north London concert halls.

George King, a gregarious and sociable fellow, was making a

name for himself as one of the founders of *The Tatler* and the very popular magazine *Sketch*. In 1900, he joined forces with the publishers Cyril and Hugh Spottiswoode and Briscoe Eyre to start a new illustrated weekly journal called *The Sphere*, a journal that was destined to be a great success.

CHAPTER SIXTEEN

Final years

F emale military nurses again saw action in Egypt and Sudan between 1882 and 1885 when thirty-five women were sent to the region. Improved hospital conditions and the establishment of training schools had begun to attract educated, middle-class young ladies who began to see nursing as one of the few chances to escape their narrow and restricted role in Victorian society. It was also a period of high morality, especially embracing the middle and upper classes of British society. Nevertheless, a growing social conscience began to develop and, nursing having become respectable, there was an increasing number of young women willing to dedicate themselves to helping others.

Sadly, any lessons that should have been learned from the Anglo Zulu War regarding the organization of medical care and supplies had been completely ignored or forgotten by the time the British Army next went on campaign. The war in Egypt in 1882 again showed up serious shortcomings, with supplies languishing in depots and not where they were needed. Hospital equipment was both insufficient and unsuited to the climate and the limited supplies of drugs, instruments and dressings quickly ran out. As Florence Nightingale remarked when she read the reports that were sent by her nurses: 'It is the Crimea, all over again!'

Sir Garnet Wolseley, who had been elevated to Commander-in-Chief, still championed the cause of female nurses in the Army and during his time in office the Army medical establishment gradually accepted the role that female nurses could play. He told the Committee of Enquiry into the state of military medical care: 'I think it would be desirable to call attention in the Queen's Regulations to the great advantage of procuring lady nurses at all stations, both in peace and war.'

Meanwhile, Janet kept in touch with the renamed British Red Cross and although now retired from nursing to bring up her family, she willingly delivered lectures about her exploits, which were always well received.

The movement, however, was not really developing in the same way as similar organizations abroad. John Furley and Sir Loyd-Lindsay, now Lord Wantage, were increasingly at odds over whether or not there should be a permanent body ready to answer any call for help rather than one that met only as a reaction to a crisis. Furthermore, Furley felt that the Society was virtually asleep and, by its inaction, had encouraged the formation of other voluntary organizations. The reactionary Loyd-Lindsay stoutly defended his policy but he was swimming against the current of opinion that believed the British Red Cross was due for reform and a change of direction.

But it was the British Red Cross, and to Janet's relief, Dr Laseron's Deaconesses' Hospital that continued to grow, thanks to the continued support of the philanthropic Morley family. This helped cover up the fact that the Tottenham Hospital, in common with all voluntary hospitals, was constantly in debt. In May 1887, Janet travelled back to her old hospital for a special occasion. The final wing of the expanded building had been completed and was opened by the Prince and Princess of Wales. Among the distinguished guests was Pastor G. Fliedner, the son of Theodor, who had founded the original Deaconesses' Institution at Kaiserswerth that had inspired the nursing movement. From the date of the royal visit, the Tottenham Hospital was named the Prince of Wales' General Hospital. Soon after, Dr Laseron became seriously ill which removed him from the running of the hospital.

In March 1894 a meeting was held in London to propose the establishment of a more aggressive Women's Volunteer Medical Staff Corps. Not only would the recruits be expected to nurse the sick but they would also be instructed in rifle shooting and marching drills. They would be self-sufficient in cooking and driving carriages and would be taught how to repair harnesses, carriages, and tents and to shoe horses. What intrigued public opinion the most, however, was the mode of dress that was proposed. A divided skirt had few supporters but there was almost unanimous disapproval for the new knickerbockers decorated with military stripes and braiding.

The whole concept provoked an outcry and satirical magazines like *Punch* had a field day. It even moved Sister Janet to deliver a lecture on the subject at the Conference Hall in Westminster in May 1894. Having told her enthralled audience of her dreadful experiences during the Russo-Turkish war, she went on to attack this outbreak of militant feminism:

If this movement has for its object the parading of certain ambitious young ladies with our volunteer regiments, gaited in slim masculine attire, there is nothing much to be said. If, on the other hand, they in all seriousness propose to go on the battlefield with arms in their hands, either as bearers or combatants, I tell them that the scheme is ridiculous. These martial young ladies have little idea of the horrors of war, of the passion and cruelty exhibited during the combat. Trying enough it is to a woman to follow the army in its arduous marches, to sleep perhaps in open carts on a snowy night, to endure all sorts of hardships, including perhaps insufficient food – work all day long without rest, and with no time for refreshment, receiving and tending the wounded – but only a man's strength and a soldier's training is equal to the task these young ladies would so lightly undertake.

Soldiers in war look upon the Red Cross Sister as an angel of mercy, ready to succour friend and foe alike; but how would a woman be regarded who unsexes herself, as it were, and, dressed in masculine attire, with arms in her hands, essays to share the combat? How will she fare when the fearful hand-to-hand fight is raging?

I have seen men come from the combat, a little while before the serried array, now a motley crowd, maddened with battle, clothes tattered and torn, faces blackened with powder and stained with blood, eyes glaring forth the fury of wild beasts. How would your lady volunteer fare then? Will she look for any distinction in the treatment of the sexes? And what would her fate be as a prisoner of war to savage Cossack or brutal Bashi Bazook, to fierce Zulu or cruel and crafty Afghan?

There is plenty of work for woman to do in nursing and tending the wounded – work for which she is more fitted than the other, and work more worthy of her; but, as bearers of the wounded on the field of battle, women would be in the way, and, indeed unless exceptionally strong, physically unsuited for the work – work that would far better be performed by men.

In Janet's speech, she remembered Dr Laseron who had been seriously ill for some time and sadly died the previous month in April 1894. How proud he would have been of this gentle girl he had trained, and who had now become the indomitable and courageous woman who was a leader of her profession.

This speech was well received and Janet went on to give a number of lectures in and around London of her experiences as a war nurse in the Balkans and Zululand. She always wore her uniform, medal and awards when speaking. The *North Finchley Newspaper* described her presentation as being delivered in a 'simple and unaffected, but nevertheless effective manner'.

For two decades the debate dragged on with the Society sending help and comforts to a number of minor wars that flickered briefly during this period. Finally, at the end of 1898, the first permanent Central Joint Red Cross Committee was set up which would spend the years of peace preparing for war. The Army was now also ready to accept the Red Cross as a supplement to its own medical service and almost immediately it was put to the test with the outbreak of the Anglo-Boer War in 1899.

Unfortunately, the Boer War exposed the still unresolved inadequacies of military medical care, and blatant disregard for basic cleanliness caused celebrated figures like Arthur Conan-Doyle and William Burdett-Coutts to write scathing reports of the poor standards of hygiene and the numbers of unnecessary deaths through disease.

By the turn of the century, female nursing was increasingly being accepted by the military and, as women gradually agitated for greater recognition, so a more militant faction sprang up. The Ladies' Volunteer Movement outraged not only the male establishment but dismayed most women, including Sister Janet. She had deeply held views about the conduct of nurses and felt that militancy had no place in the profession. Like Florence Nightingale, Janet was fully prepared to argue for the position and influence of nurses treating casualties of war on the battlefield and at home in peace time.

George and Janet King were now settled in the Purley area of south Croydon, part of the new sub-urbanization of London. George had been appointed managing director of both *The Tatler* and *The Sphere* and life was very comfortable. Through his business connections, George and Janet enjoyed a full social life and received numerous invitations to dinners and balls. As musical as ever, Janet loved attending concerts and all the social functions that were now part of her life.

In 1901, Queen Victoria died and Sister Janet was invited to the state funeral. Proudly wearing her decorations, she renewed old acquaintanceships from her Zulu War days, including the recently retired Lord Wolseley. She was also introduced to the new Commander-in-Chief, Lord Roberts.

In March 1904, Sister Janet was once again in the public eye when the newspapers and *Ladies' Field* reported that she had received another award. Somewhat belatedly, the Russian government bestowed on her the Russian Imperial Order of the Red Cross in recognition of her service during the war of 1877–78. *The Times* reported the award on 14 March 1904. Once again, her story was retold to an admiring public: 'Mrs George King, who was awarded the decoration of the Royal Red Cross by her late Majesty for her services in the Zulu War, has just received from the Russian Government the decoration of the Russian Red Cross for her services in the Russo-Turkish War of 1877–8.'

1910 saw the deaths of two of the people who inspired Janet to devote her early life to the care of sick and wounded soldiers. Florence Nightingale, after years of physical decline, passed away on 13 August. On 30 October, Henri Dunant died at the age of eighty-two, outliving his nemesis Gustav Moynier by just nine weeks. Sadly, Janet was about to join them. Some years before the demise of the two greatest inspirations of her career, Janet had realized all was not well with her and a diagnosis of cancer was made. The shock of such news is always difficult for anyone to cope with, as Janet knew only too well. Quietly and resolutely Janet prepared to face the ultimate test that lay ahead of her. She submitted to surgery several times in the attempt to try to remove the malignant growth and was tenderly nursed by the Laseron trained girls at the Tottenham Hospital. Often at night when the pain-filled hours left her wakeful, she would think about the past and the times when she had been a young probationer on this very ward. In her mind's eye she could, no doubt, visualize the many friends she had made there and hear the echoes of their merry laughter.

The last known letter of Janet Wells to her daughter Elsie and son-in-law Tom:

9 Wood View
Furze Lane
Purley

16 Oct 1909

My darling Elsie and Tom,

This is to wish you both many happy returns of your wedding day.

We have all been thinking of this time last year & all the excitement. Thank goodness you had better weather than this, it has not stopped raining all day.

I am thankful today – I am feeling rather better tonight. I am not to have that operation but if other pain is cleared up I will explain it all to you when I see you.

I am still in bed but if I am still feeling better and free from pain tomorrow, I shall get up.

Father has gone to Southend to see his mother.

We shall expect you on Monday.

Wishing you both all the happiness as mother would wish you in a picture with much love,

Your ever loving mother

Janet H King

When there was finally nothing more that could be done, George came and took Janet home to die with her family around her. The latter years of her life had been spent at their country home at Furze Hill, Purley in Surrey. Elsie was expecting her first baby and Janet hoped to see her grandchild before she died. Sadly, only nine days before her first grandson was born, Janet slipped into the twilight world between life and death. With larger doses of morphine having to be administered to her she began to hallucinate and spoke as if to those she had nursed and cared for in Bulgaria and South Africa. There was Osman Pasha with the Tsarevitch, Cossacks and fleeting glimpses of Bashi Bazooks. Harry Peterson and King Cetshwayo passed by and she spoke of Dr Fitzmaurice who, she thought, was in earnest conversation with the Zulu Sangoma and Surgeon General Ross. As she deteriorated, her final visions were of her fellow nurses and doctors, then friends and family.

After the years of pain and surgery, which she bore with typical stoicism, Janet finally succumbed to her illness on 6 June 1911. She was only fifty-three. The funeral was a modest family affair at Brandon Hill Cemetery in Purley. This was in contrast to the extensive and glowing tributes she received in the many obituaries that appeared right across the country. (See Appendix H for *The Times* obituary.) *The Times*, *Daily Mail* and *Daily Telegraph* were all fulsome in their praise of her career. *The Chronicle* went so far as to say: 'The late Mrs King was well known as a nurse; in fact, after the late Florence Nightingale, Sister Janet, as Mrs King was known, takes the premier place among the Red Cross nurses.'

The provincial papers also carried her obituary under headings that included – *Death of Famous Nurse . . . Death of Red Cross Heroine . . . Death of a Brave Nurse . . . a Heroine of the Battlefields* or simply, *Sister Janet*. From London to Aberdeen and from Cork to Birmingham, the papers sang her praises. *The Ladies' Field* ended their tribute with the words: 'But no woman of her generation will see the announcement of her death today without a grateful remembrance of her services to her country and her sex.'

So passed away a remarkable woman who, without being in any way militant, did much through her quiet bravery and dedication to further the female cause in medical care. Within four years of Janet's death, when the world was plunged into the first of the catastrophic twentieth century wars, women would finally be accepted as an essential part of the medical profession.

The Royal Red Cross
Parliamentary Papers

1. Balmoral

To Mr Childers. The War Office.

The Queen thinks it would be very desirable to establish a decoration for nurses who are employed on active service, and for those who assist them at home, and commands me to give you her views on the subject.

Miss Nightingale and a very few of the nurses under her and associated with her got a badge after the Crimean War: but that was only for that special occasion and very expensive, and not in the form of an Order, which the Queen now wishes to establish.

The badge or cross need not be of an expensive nature, and might be worn with a ribbon on the shoulder.

It should be awarded to nurses sent out by the War Office and also to others who have made themselves useful in the field, such as the Bloemfontein Sisters, in whose praise you wrote to the Queen last March.

Her Majesty would wish to confer this decoration on the nurses who served in the South African Wars as well as on those now in Egypt.

Sir Henry Ponsonby, Her Majesty's Private Secretary. 12th September 1882

2. To Sir Henry Ponsonby.

May I ask you to say to the Queen in reply to the command contained in your letter of the 12th instant about a decoration for nurses, that I will lose no time in considering the question, which, however, may require a good deal of inquiry and thought. Do you happen to be able to tell me, or to tell me where I can obtain, any information of the St. Katherine's foundation, of which William Ashley used to be the treasurer, and which, at his death, was, I think, utilized by her Majesty's special wish, for nursing purposes, to some extent? No one here has any information on the subject.

Mr Childers. The War Office. 14th September 1882

3. To Mr Childers. The War Office.

I did not mean to convey to you that the Queen preferred a 'decoration' for nurses to an 'order' because I do not clearly understand the difference.

Both must be conferred under certain regulations, and both are honours given by the Queen.

Your proposal that the cross should be granted to nurses engaged in time of peace is a good one.

It is considered very desirable that 'those who have assisted at home' should be included.

Would you take into consideration the rules it would be desirable to make for this order or decoration?

The Queen has had a Cross made as a model. Her Majesty is not quite pleased with it and will make some alterations. I send it to you to look at.

Sir Henry Ponsonby, Her Majesty's Private Secretary. 23rd October 1882

N.B. Those who have assisted at home would include the Queen and the Princesses.

4. To Sir Henry Ponsonby. Cantley.

I send you a draft of the Royal Warrant which I propose to submit in due course for her Majesty's approval, establishing the new decoration for nurses.

The title has been a difficulty with us: but, upon the whole, I don't think that anything can be better devised than the 'Royal Red Cross'.

The Royal Red Cross has now been adopted by the whole Christian world as the symbol of aid to the sick and wounded in war; and it is the badge of our own Army Hospital Corps. You will observe that it may be conferred on princesses or any ladies for special services in providing for aid to sick and wounded soldiers, and on nursing sisters, whether serving in the field or in hospital.

I would strongly urge that the statutes of St Katherine's Hospital should be simultaneously altered so as to admit of pensions being granted to a limited number of the new décorees. This would have a very good effect in showing that the object is both titular and substantial.

Mr Childers. The War Office. 12th December 1882.

The Nursing Record & Nursing World. 7 October 1899

The decoration was instituted by Her Majesty the Queen, on St George's Day 1883, as a recognition of 'zeal and devotion in providing for and nursing sick and wounded sailors, soldiers, and others with the Army in the field, on board ships, or in hospitals'. It is usually conferred by the Queen in person, a kindly act which is much appreciated by the recipient of this honour.

The Royal Red Cross is, we believe, at present, the only decoration bestowed by her Majesty in recognition of women's work, and it has been a source of pleasure to us and to many others to see, in recent times, the names of nurses in the New Year's and Birthday Honours lists as the recipients of the Royal Red Cross. We hope that eventually a decoration will be instituted for women who have distinguished themselves in other branches of work. Women are now entering largely into public life, and performing services of public utility, and they, in common with men, appreciate the recognition of work well done.

Foreign as well as British subjects are eligible for the Royal Red Cross, but so far those, other than British subjects, upon whom it has been conferred, are Royal ladies.

The British Journal of Nursing 20 November 1915

A Royal Warrant dated November 10th was gazetted on Tuesday night for enlarging the Order of the Royal Red Cross, instituted by Queen Victoria on St. George's day 1883 'For zeal and devotion in providing for and nursing sick and wounded sailors, soldiers, and others with the army in the field, on board ships, or in hospitals.'

The decoration is now divided into two classes. It is provided that the First Class shall consist of a Cross, enamelled red, edged with gold, having on the arms thereof the words, *Faith, Hope, Charity*, with the date of the institution of the decoration; the centre having thereon in relief the Royal and Imperial Effigy. On the reverse thereof the Royal and Imperial Cipher and Crown shall be shown in relief on the centre.

The Second Class shall consist of a Cross which shall be of the same size and form as in the First Class, but shall be of frosted silver and shall have superimposed thereon a Maltese Cross enamelled red not exceeding half its dimensions, the centre having thereon in relief the Royal and Imperial Effigy. The reverse shall have on the arms thereof the words Faith, Hope, Charity, and the date of the institution of the original decoration, and shall bear in the centre in relief the Royal and Imperial Cipher and Crown.

The Cross in either class shall be attached to a dark blue ribbon and edged red, of one inch in width, tied in a bow and worn on the left shoulder.

The First Lord of the Admiralty, as well as the Secretary of State for War, is empowered to recommend for the decoration any members of the Nursing Services or other persons engaged in nursing duties, whether subjects or foreign persons, for special devotion and competency with the Army in the field or in the naval and military hospitals.

The awards in the first class are not to exceed 2 per cent, and in the second class 5 per cent, of the total establishment of nurses, save in exceptional circumstances. Recipients of the First Class will be designated 'Members of the Royal Red Cross' and will be entitled to the letters RRC following their names. And recipients of the Second Class will be designated 'Associates of the Royal Red Cross', and will be entitled to the letters ARRC following their names.

Honorary membership and associateship may be conferred on Royal or other ladies for cause shown.

The British Journal of Nursing 26 June 1920

The little bronze cross, of no intrinsic value, bearing the words 'For Valour' instituted by Queen Victoria on January 29th 1856 as the decoration of the Victoria Cross – is probably more coveted than any other; for it indicates that the wearer showed conspicuous bravery, initiative and resourcefulness 'where valiant men were all' – under circumstances of extreme peril. So far, it has only been awarded to men, but the recent war (Zulu War of 1879) has proved beyond question that women are capable, not only of enduring danger unflinchingly and heroically, but of voluntarily assuming responsibilities which involve exposure to, and disregard of, great dangers, from motives of patriotism, or in order to save life.

Prior to the South African War (Boer War 1900) the Royal Red Cross was regarded as the Nurses' Victoria Cross. It also was instituted by Queen Victoria, on St George's Day 1883, 'For zeal and devotion in providing for, and nursing, sick and wounded sailors, soldiers, and others with the army in the field, on board ship or in hospitals'. It was only rarely awarded and conferred real and well-maintained distinction on its possessor.

Appendix B

Evangelical Protestant Deaconesses' Institution and Training Hospital, The Green, London. Dr M. A. H. Laseron, Hon. Director

The Prince of Wales' General Hospital originated in the Evangelical Protestant Deaconesses' Institution and Training Hospital, founded by Dr. Laseron with help from John Morley of Upper Clapton and his brother Samuel. Avenue House, on the south-east side of the Green, was converted and opened, with a new hospital block, in 1868; the old house was replaced in 1881 and further extensions included the John Morley wing, opened in 1887. The institution had fourteen offshoots, including two hospitals in Ireland, at the time of Laseron's death in 1894, whereupon subscriptions declined. Under a Charity Commissioners' Scheme, effective from 1899, the voluntary deaconesses surrendered control to a committee and were replaced by paid, certificated nurses. To mark the change from a training centre to a general hospital for the district, the institution was renamed Tottenham Hospital. Further additions were made and, to emphasize that it served a wide area, the name was again changed to the Prince of Wales' General hospital in 1907. After adjoining property had been bought in 1917, additions, included a building for outpatients, opened in 1932, and a new home for fifty-five nurses. In 1972 the hospital lay within the North-East Metropolitan region and was administered by Tottenham Hospital management committee. It had 200 beds and dealt with acute cases.

From: *Tottenham: Public services, A History of the County of Middlesex*: Volume V: Hendon, Kingsbury.

APPENDIX C

Military General Hospitals

The Military Nursing Service was born after a long and very difficult labour. In 1861 Florence Nightingale had recommended Jane Shaw Stewart, the aristocratic daughter of Sir Michael Shaw Stewart, 6th Baronet of Ardgowan, for the post of Superintendent of Nurses at the Woolwich Hospital. She moved to Netley on 25 May 1868. After a very unhappy and tempestuous period, when the autocratic Jane Shaw Stewart attempted to impose her will on the Military Nursing Service, the War Office instituted an enquiry into the conduct of the Superintendent General of Nursing at Netley and the bad state of nursing. The setting up of the enquiry was the culmination of the continuous series of claims, counter claims, accusations and recriminations that had accompanied Jane Shaw Stewart's career in Military General Hospitals. Colonel Wilbraham, the Military Governor, expressed the opinion that she exhibited a violent temper, and an imperious and inflammatory manner, which provoked complaints from nurses, orderlies, medical officers and even patients.

Florence Nightingale believed Jane Stewart's hints that some of Colonel Wilbraham's resentments originated outside the hospital. He had felt maligned when the aristocratic Superintendent General declined to socialize with his sisters or accept their vague offers of help on the wards.

The War Office produced a report that was not communicated to either Colonel Wilbraham or Jane Shaw Stewart. They were both sent a private letter of reprimand. More seriously, Jane failed to reach agreement with the medical officers at both Netley and Woolwich and the nurses were unable to carry out many of their duties. As she became more isolated and was unable to carry out her duties or communicate with the medical staff, she resigned to be replaced by Mrs Jane Deeble, the widow of an Army medical officer.

Lieutenants Coghill & Melvill – Saving the Colour

The story, then currently popular, was that at the moment the camp at Isandlwana was being overrun, Lieutenant Colonel Pulleine ordered Lieutenant Melvill to prevent the Queen's Colour from falling into Zulu hands by carrying it off to safety. Leaping onto his horse, he was joined by his friend, Lieutenant Coghill, who volunteered to accompany him. Then, with the banner picturesquely billowing behind them, they shot and hacked their way through the Zulu hordes until they reached the precipitous bank overlooking the Buffalo River.

After the recent rains, the river was in full spate and, in normal circumstances, crossing it at this point was unthinkable. With bloodthirsty warriors pressing closely behind, the two officers took their chances in the swift-flowing water. Coghill managed to force his horse across to the far bank but, as he looked back, he saw that Melvill had become unseated and was desperately clinging to a rock in the middle of the river. Without hesitation, Coghill turned his mount around to go to his friend's aid. A chance shot killed his horse, which collapsed and disappeared under the water. Coghill swam to Melvill and together they managed to reach the safety of the Natal bank.

The story related how the Zulus had somehow managed to cross the river and closed in on the pair. Coghill was almost lame and begged that Melvill should go on alone. Instead, Melvill half dragged his friend up the steep sides of the canyon until, exhausted and completely surrounded, they made their last defiant stand, selling their lives dearly, as the ring of dead Zulus later attested.

The reality, although dramatic enough, was somewhat more prosaic. It has never been confirmed that Melvill received any such order to save the colours but he did leave with the Colour encased in a cumbersome black leather tube just before the camp was totally overrun. Coghill left a little earlier and at no time were the two seen together during the six-mile ride across country to the Buffalo River. Here, Coghill plunged into the river and managed to cross. When he looked back, he saw Melvill clinging to the rock with another officer, Captain Higginson of the NNC. He then bravely attempted to urge his horse, which had been severely wounded by stab wounds, back into the stream until it was shot dead by the Zulus. Coghill swam to the rock and found that the exhausted Melvill had lost both his horse and the Colour. The other officer volunteered to swim for the Natal bank to find horses. Coghill and Melvill finally swam to the shore and, exhausted, slowly began to climb the steep slope.

Natives living along the Natal bank of the river then joined their Zulu cousins in harassing the fugitives and it was a band of these who went after the two officers. Coghill was badly handicapped by a sprained knee sustained during some horseplay in the officers' mess a couple of weeks before. The two thoroughly exhausted men were finally caught and quickly dispatched. There was no last-ditch stand as Melvill's revolver was useless; the cylinder had fallen out.

There was no doubting the bravery of the two men, Coghill for going back into the river to help Melvill, and Melvill for not leaving his lame friend. Wolseley, ever critical of officers whom he considered to have deserted their men, fiercely wrote:

I am sorry that both of these men were not killed with their men at Isandlwana instead of where they were. I don't like the idea of officers escaping on horseback when their men on foot are killed. Heroes have been made of men like Melvill and Coghill, who, taking advantage of their horses,

166

bolted from the scene of the action to save their lives, it is monstrous making heroes of those who saved or attempted to save their lives by bolting.

Wolseley's views did not prevail and Melvill and Coghill remain among the most heroic figures of the Zulu War.

For further detailed analysis of the two officers' escape from Isandlwana see Greaves, Adrian, *Isandlwana*, Cassell, 2002.

APPENDIX E

An overview of the
Battle of Rorke's Drift
22–23 January 1879

In 1879 Lord Chelmsford's disastrous invasion of Zululand and his unexpected defeat by the Zulu army at Isandlwana shook Victorian Britain. The nation desperately needed heroes and the unprecedented award of eleven Victoria Crosses and five Distinguished Conduct Medals for the heroic defence of nearby Rorke's Drift ensured that an insignificant skirmish, bravely fought, transformed disaster into a great British victory. In 1964 the celebrated film *Zulu* immortalized the legend of tenacious redcoats and dashing officers doggedly resisting overwhelming odds; the glory of the British Empire lived on.

On 11 January 1879 Lord Chelmsford led the British invasion force against Zululand, crossing the Buffalo River border at Rorke's Drift. This act of war against a friendly neighbour was unauthorized by the home government but Chelmsford believed he could secure Zululand before news of his invasion reached England. Chelmsford's invasion force of 4,709 men advanced from their picturesque supply depot at Rorke's Drift, quietly nestling under the Oskarsberg Hill, and made camp ten miles inside Zululand at Isandlwana Hill prior to attacking the gathering Zulu army.

168

Rorke's Drift boasted two insignificant buildings; Surgeon Reynolds' temporary hospital with thirty patients and a storehouse containing the invading column's supplies, supported by Captain Stevenson with 300 black auxiliaries from Natal for labouring duties.

On 22 January the detachment at Rorke's Drift included Lieutenant Bromhead and 100 soldiers of B Company 2/24 (Warwickshire) Regiment. His senior NCO was twenty-four year-old Colour Sergeant Bourne. An engineer officer, Lieutenant Chard, had arrived at Rorke's Drift the day before; all were under the command of Major Spalding.

After sunrise on 22 January, Chard rode to nearby Isandlwana camp to ascertain his orders. Meanwhile, the Zulus had decoyed Chelmsford into believing the Zulu army was approaching Isandlwana and, overnight, Chelmsford marched half his force off to make battle. But the approaching Zulu army had slipped unobserved into a hidden valley three miles from the unprotected camp's flank. There were no orders for Chard, who observed massing Zulus advancing on the British position. He galloped back to Rorke's Drift where he alerted Spalding. Leaving Chard in command, Spalding set off to Helpmekaar for reinforcements declaring, 'Nothing will happen, and I shall be back again this evening, early'. Reassured by Spalding, Chard returned to his riverside tent for lunch without warning Bromhead, whose soldiers were avoiding the heat of the day by sleeping or haunting the cooking area.

Chelmsford's marching force was twelve miles from the unprepared British camp when the massed Zulu army attacked Isandlwana. Within two hours, the camp was destroyed and 1,400 troops lay massacred and disembowelled.

Led by Prince Dabulamanzi, the Zulu reserve of 4,500 Zulus then crossed into British Natal near Rorke's Drift and divided into raiding impis. One impi encountered Major Spalding and forced his relief column back to Helpmekaar; another impi discovered the weakly defended Mission Station at Rorke's Drift. Alerted to the approaching Zulus, Bromhead urgently dispatched a rider with a note to the garrison at Helpmekaar.

Sir,

Intelligence has just reached camp that the camp at Isandula Hill is taken by the enemy.

Bromhead

Bromhead organized a hastily erected defensive wall of mealie sacks and biscuit boxes, strengthened by two upturned wagons, between the storehouse and the hospital. The hospital was barricaded and loop-holed for the anxiously awaiting soldiers to fire through. Colour Sergeant Bourne took a skirmishing party to delay the approaching Zulus. As the marauding Zulus approached Rorke's Drift, Captain Stevenson's terrified black auxiliaries deserted, hotly followed by Stevenson and his white NCOs. The men of B Company fired a volley into the fleeing deserters and a Corporal Anderson fell dead. Bromhead hastily directed six soldiers to defend the hospital and sealed the doors and windows with sacks and boxes as the Zulus spread out into their classic attacking 'horns' formation, progressively forcing Bourne's skirmishers back to the post.

At 4.30 p.m. the Zulus charged the two buildings, only to be met by withering volley-fire from 100 British rifles; many warriors fell during this concentrated charge. Those behind the Zulu casualties jumped over them but their bravery was wasted, as they were unable to climb the barricade, now awash with slippery blood. With no time to reload their rifles, the soldiers fought with their bayonets fixed and, although the Zulus relished close combat, British bayonets forced their retreat. Such tactics were new to the soldiers who were now fighting for their lives. Scores of dead and wounded Zulus soon lay several deep around the position.

Zulu marksmen commenced sniping into the backs of Bromhead's soldiers from the Oskarsberg; fortunately they were poor shots and casualties were few. Close-range volleys blasted each Zulu attack and those who survived could only run onto the waiting blooded bayonets. Chard and Bromhead calmly controlled the outpost and, when a gap appeared, one or other would step forward to assist the fight, ensuring each wave of Zulus was forced to retreat. When Commissariat Officer Dalton

170

was shot at close range, he handed his rifle to Chard before collapsing, Surgeon Reynolds dressed the wound and, within minutes, Dalton was back on his feet encouraging the defenders. Unable to reach the hospital, Surgeon Reynolds bravely issued ammunition along the line.

Four of Chard's men were now seriously wounded and one determined Zulu rush finally forced the soldiers to abandon the outer position and withdraw within the inner wall of boxes next to the storehouse. Chard could no longer communicate with those trapped in the hospital, forty yards away and surrounded by Zulus.

A soldier shouted that he saw marching redcoats approaching from Helpmekaar. Some of the men cheered, which confused the Zulus; they momentarily withdrew but no relieving troops came and the Zulus re-grouped for the next assault. Chard wrote of this incident:

It is very strange that this report should have arisen amongst us, for the two companies 24th Regiment from Helpmekaar did come down to the foot of the hill, but not, I believe, in sight of us. They marched back to Helpmekaar on the report of Rorke's Drift having fallen.

With darkness falling, the Zulus attacked the hospital's barricaded doors and windows, grabbing at the soldiers' rifles as they fired through the loopholes. Then the hospital caught fire; Private Hook wrote, 'We were like rats in a trap'. The Zulus began clawing at the barricaded doors forcing the defenders through to the far room, its high window overlooking Chard's position. In the glare of the hospital flames Chard saw the defenders lowering the hospital patients to the ground. The Zulus were only yards away when Chard ordered covering fire and called for volunteers to bring the patients to safety. Although wounded, Private Hitch and Corporal Allen immediately volunteered; the two raced to and from the hospital, each time carrying a patient. The hospital was quickly vacated. The terrifying battle in the darkness, thick smoke and deafening noise had lasted over two hours.

The final desperate fight for survival now began. Drawn by the flames and sounds of constant firing, Zulu reinforcements arrived. Facing imminent death and with hand-to-hand fighting around them, a dozen weary soldiers constructed a final redoubt of mealie sacks. The wounded were placed inside the 'last post' position and Chard detailed marksmen to occupy the upper rampart. Thankfully, the Zulus' enthusiasm for close combat waned and after midnight their attacks reduced to half-hearted probes. Prince Dabulamanzi's men had suffered enormous casualties with nothing to show for their undisputed bravery. At dawn the exhausted Zulus collected themselves together and, leaving over 300 of their warriors dead, they retreated towards Zululand.

The soldiers were all suffering from bruising and burns caused by constantly firing their Martini-Henry rifles. Pools of congealed blood bore witness to the death-throes of both sides and the whole area was littered with bodies, spears, empty ammunition boxes and clusters of spent ammunition cases. The soldiers contemplated the Zulu dead, sometimes five deep. Dying and wounded warriors were given the *coup de grâce* by bayonet; there was no malice, neither side took prisoners.

At 9 a.m. Chelmsford and his survivors reached Rorke's Drift where 'the occupants received the General with three cheers'. Chelmsford and his staff were shocked by the carnage that greeted them. Hundreds of bodies lay around the Mission Station and within the burnt-out hospital building. Chelmsford thanked the survivors for their endeavours before departing to report the defeat of his force and annihilation of a famous British regiment.

After the tragedy of Isandlwana, Chelmsford described the survival of Rorke's Drift as a 'gleam of sunshine'. Victory at Rorke's Drift successfully neutralized his defeat at Isandlwana although the Army viewed the event as a minor skirmish. News of awards provoked annoyance through the ranks and contempt from General Wolseley, from which many survivors would later suffer. Both Chard and Bromhead were promoted but their careers then floundered. Encouraged by the popular press, Chelmsford and the politicians successfully used victory at Rorke's Drift to countervail Isandlwana.

Today, Rorke's Drift ranks as one of the most popular British battlefields in the world.

It was the only Anglo Zulu War battlefield that was attended by any of the nurses sent out from England. Nurse Janet Wells, aged nineteen years, was originally posted to the most northern hospital at Utrecht, a base garrison for the Northern Column of Colonel Wood VC. The garrison there saw no direct action although Nurse Wells treated casualties from the nearby battles of Hlobane and Khambula. Following the declaration of peace she then moved on to Rorke's Drift where she attended the holding garrison at Rorke's Drift, which had been without medical attention for several weeks.

For further detailed analysis of the battle at Rorke's Drift see Greaves, Adrian, *Rorke's Drift*, Cassell, 2002.

Press reports mentioning Sister Janet in South Africa

From *Times of Natal* 13 August 1879

During the last few days Utrecht has shown more than ordinary signs of life. On Saturday a body of Wood's Irregulars, under the command of Loraine White, marched into town to be disbanded. They were drawn up in front of the Landrost's Office, and executed a dance. They were then encamped on the veld south of the town.

Today (5th) Oham left with some of his men to join the expedition which is to endeavour to bring in Manyanoba, the rebel chief from the Pongola District.

That part of the cemetery where lie the bodies of those of the Imperial forces who have died in Utrecht during the present war, has been enclosed within a stone wall. Sods have been laid down, and a slab has been erected by the 4th Kings Own to those of their comrades who are buried therein. We are soon to lose the 4th Regiment, who are to proceed to Luneburg, and will be relieved by the 24th and Dragoons, whose head-quarters are to be in Utrecht.

The sick and wounded who are still in hospital have now the kind attentions and experienced services of a lady nurse (Miss Wells) who has placed herself at the disposal of the Stafford House Committee.

From *The Natal Witness* 26 July 1879

We must not omit to make a short reference to the excellent way in which the Sisters of Mercy, attached to these two hospitals, (Addington & Durban) are doing work which they have undertaken. Sisters Annette and Mary have been stationed at these hospitals, and they have been joined by four sisters sent out with some other ladies from the Stafford House Committee. Then there are the two sisters from St Catherine's, Cape Town. Six nurses of great experience arrived some days since from Netley Hospital and they commenced their duty last Tuesday. The latter is perhaps the largest military hospital in the world. The six ladies are under Lady Superintendent Deeble.

From *The Daily Telegraph* 30 October 1879

After the parade of Sept. 11, of the 24th Regiment, at which the Commander-in-Chief affixed the Victoria Cross to the breasts of Major Bromhead and Private Jones for their share in the defence of Rorke's Drift, his Excellency visited the hospital, and made a minute examination of the condition of the patients, at the close of which, he expressed his satisfaction to the medical officers (Somerford and Fitzmaurice) in charge, and exchanged a few words with Sister Janet, of the Stafford House Committee, whose care and attention to the sick are well worthy of notice, and have been most gratefully appreciated by those among whom she has been ministering. There was one outlying shed which escaped his notice; but in front of it, on the ground in their blankets, were some unfortunates whom he would have pitied; could he have seen them – six Zulu prisoners, wounded at the battle of Kambula, who have been here ever since March. Hitherto they have had a surgeon in attendance who spoke their language, but now they are under the charge of a kind-hearted orderly, who, when I passed by, was trying to make them understand his meaning by a free use of pigeon English. They are all badly wounded, and three, at least, ought to have their legs amputated, but they will not submit to an operation, and the result is not doubtful.

From *The Daily Telegraph* 23 October 1879

The P.M.O. Surgeon-General, General Woolfryes, has issued an order for the Government nurses under Mrs Deeble to prepare to return to England. The Stafford House Sisters will no doubt follow their fellow-workers very speedily, and Surgeon-General Ross has arrived at Newcastle on his way to Utrecht, which is the furthest point northwards to which the operations of agents of the committee have extended. In order to close the accounts of the committee, Surgeon Stoker has been attached to the force of Swazis and others who have been placed under the orders of Colonel Villiers, but as there is little likelihood of there being any armed opposition or any wounded, he will probably soon be on his way down to Durban. Of the general utility of the work which the Stafford House Sisters have done, the best witnesses are the grateful soldiers whom they have tended, and the subscribers may rest satisfied that no money was ever laid out to more advantage than that which has been confided to Surgeon-General Ross and Mr. Stoker. The seven sisters who arrived at Durban on July 13 were immediately distributed among the hospitals along the frontiers. Sister Ruth and Sister Elizabeth were assigned to the Auxiliary Base Hospital at Durban, where they are still employed; Sister Mary and Sister Annette were sent to the Head-quarters Hospital at Pietermaritzburg; Sister Edith and Sister Emma went up to Ladysmith; and Sister Janet made her way up to the General Field Hospital at Utrecht, and among sick and wounded, cases of fever and dysentery, and all the suffering which war entails, these excellent women have been toiling with the most admirable results, winning the praise and admiration of those who have been associated with them in their self-denying and never-ending duties. Surgeon-General Ross expects to be back at Ladysmith, on his way to Durban, on Sept. 20, unless there appears to be some occasion for the services of the sisters arising out of troubles in the Transvaal, and in all probability he will be on his way back to England, with the sisters under his charge, by the end of the present month.

Appendix G

Major Ronald Ross of the Royal Army Medical Corps spent most of his working life trying to solve the 'great problem' of how malaria affected soldiers. He knew that soldiers throughout the British Empire were dying in unacceptable numbers from fever and, being astute, he also knew that whoever solved the problem would reap the rewards. He sought to resolve the problem in Europe, through Africa to India but finally found the solution by looking through a microscope, eventually receiving the Nobel Prize in 1920.

The Times obituary of Sister Janet

Saturday June 10, 1911

The death took place on Tuesday last at Wood View, Purley, of Mrs. George King (Sister Janet, Royal Red Cross and Imperial Cross of Russia).

Janet Helen King was the daughter of Prof. Benjamin Wells, ARAM., and was born in London. When she was but 18 years of age, deeply impressed by the accounts of the suffering of those fighting in the struggle between Servian Independence and Turkish supremacy, and impelled by a high sense of duty, she entered the Protestant Deaconesses' Institution to be trained for nursing the sick and wounded in war. Quickly becoming proficient, she was selected as one of a party of nine sent out by that institution to assist in nursing the sick and wounded engaged in the war between Russia and Turkey in 1877–78. The party proceeded to Bukarest under orders to the Russian National Red Cross Society, and were there directed to join the army of the Tsarevitch, which was operating on the Lom. Travelling by railway as far as Fratesti, they journeyed thence in rough carts to Semnitza and crossed the Danube by the bridge of boats to Sistova, where they waited for an escort to Vardin.

179

Sistova was at the time of their arrival not only crowded with wounded from Plevna, but was being ravaged by typhus, so that the sisters found plenty of work to do while they were detained there. The escort having been provided, the sisters continued their journey in rough carts, suffering on the way from much privation from the bitter cold.

At Vardin they found their services sorely needed, and throughout the winter months they worked from early morning until late at night. Sister Janet was placed in charge of 200 patients who lay in huts scattered among the hills. More than once as she passed from hut to hut on her daily mission she was attacked by the wild dogs, and twice she was attacked by Bashi-Bazook patients. Communication across the Danube was stopped, coarse black bread was the only diet, and there was no news from home. When the army of Suleiman Pasha was driven back on Rustchuk the sisters were sent there, experiencing another terrible journey. Half of them were down with typhus, and Sister Janet was so severely tried in nursing her companions that on the capitulation of Rustchuk she returned to England, having been decorated for her services with the Imperial Order of the Red Cross of Russia.

Sister Janet was appointed Superintendent of the hospital at Newcastle-upon-Tyne, and was selected by the Stafford House Committee for service with Surgeon General Ross in the Zulu War. At Utrecht, 3,200 sick and wounded passed through her hands, many of her patients being Zulus. Sir Garnet Wolseley, when he visited the hospital at Utrecht, personally thanked Sister Janet for her work, and on the conclusion of the war, she was awarded the South Africa medal and received from Queen Victoria the decoration of the Royal Red Cross for 'the special devotion and competency displayed in nursing duties with her majesty's troops'.

Sister Janet married Mr George King in 1882.

The funeral service takes place today at St. Mark's, Purley at half past 2.

Similar obituaries appeared in the following national newspapers and magazines:

The Daily Chronicle
The Daily Mail
The Queen
The Chronicle
The Broad Arrow
The Gentlewoman
The News of the World
Lady's Pictorial
The Ladies' Field
Army and Navy Gazette
Nursing Mirror

and in most regional newspapers, across the depth and breath of the United Kingdom.

Further details about the Anglo Zulu War and its personalities can be found at www.anglozuluwar.com or by contacting *The Anglo Zulu War Historical Society* at –

The AZWHS
Woodbury House
Woodchurch Road
Tenterden
Kent
TN30 7AE

Tel: 01580-764189

Family details

The Wells Family

(Taken from the 1881 Census)

99 St Stephens Avenue
Shepherds Bush
London

Name	Age	Relation to Family Head	Rank or profession
Benjamin Wells	54	Head	Professor Music
Elizabeth	54	Wife	
Kate	29	Daughter	Unmarried
Janet Helen	22	Daughter	Unmarried
Ada	20	Daughter	Teacher Music
Eva	18	Daughter	Teacher Music
Elizabeth	16	Daughter	Unmarried
Harry	25	Son	Architect
Augustus	23	Son	Architect
Clifford	13	Son	Scholar

The King Family

(Taken from the 1901 census)

St Heliers
Cromartie Road
Islington
London

Name Where born	Relation to Head of Family	Condition as to Marriage	Profession
George King Camberwell	Head	Married	Newspaper Manager and Director of public companies
Janet H. King Shepherds Bush	Wife	Married	
Daisy H. King	Daughter	Aged 8	W. Hampstead
Elizabeth Doughty Islington	Governess	Single	Governess – Domestic
Kate Meadows Suffolk	Servant	Single	Cook
Fanny Meadows Suffolk	Servant	Single	Housemaid

* property since re-developed

** property still in existence

Mr George King

(Husband of Sister Janet, from *Who's Who* 1933)

Director and founder of *The Sphere* and *Tatler*; Chairman of *Technical Journals Ltd.*, proprietor of *The Architect's Journal* and *The Architectural Review*. Winner of the £500 prize competition given by *Tit Bits* for best scheme of National Old Age Pensions.
  Recreations; Golf and fishing.
  Clubs; Devonshire and Constitutional
  Died 12th July 1933.

Known addresses of Sister Janet

99, St Stephen's Avenue, Shepherds Bush, London (Childhood and pre-marriage)**

St Heliers, Cromartie Road, Islington, London (Married)*

Vardin, Bexley Heath, Kent (Married)*

Woodend, Furze Hill, Purley, Surrey (retired to and died at this address)**

Buried at Brandon Hill cemetery, Purley, Surrey.

Bibliography

Anderson, D., *The Balkan Volunteers*, Hutchinson, 1968

Bailey, Hamilton, *Pye's Surgical Handicraft*, John Wright and Sons, nd

Bailey, Hamilton and Love, R.J. McNeill, *Short Practice of Surgery*, H.K. Lewis, nd

Best, S.H., *The Story of the British Red Cross*, Cassell, 1938

Blair Brown, D., *Surgical Experiences in the Zulu and Transvaal Wars, 1879 & 1881*, Oliver & Boyd, 1883

Boissier, Pierre, *From Solferino to Tsushima*, pub. unk., 1865

Bradshaw, Ann, *The Nurse Apprentice 1860 – 1977*, Ashgate Publishers Ltd., 2001

British Orthopaedic Association, *A Historical Guide to British Orthopaedic Surgery*, nd

Bulpin, T.V., *Natal and the Zulu Country*, Books of Africa (Cape Town), 1966

Drury, Ian, *The Russo-Turkish War 1877*, Osprey, 1994

Dunant, Henri, *A Memory of Solferino*, pub. unk., 1860

Forbes, Archibald, *Memories & Studies of War & Peace*, Cassell, 1895

Funnell, Edith M., *Aids to Hygiene for Nurses*, Bailliere Tindall and Cox, 1962

Furley, John, *In Peace and War – Autobiographical Sketches*, Smith, Elder & Co., 1905

Goldsworthy, Vesna, *Inventing Ruritania*, Yale University, 1998

Gore, Surgeon Major Albert A., *Our Services Under the Crown - Ashanti War*, Bailliere, Tindall and Cox, 1879

Greaves, Adrian, *Crossing the Buffalo*, Cassell, 2005

— *Isandlwana*, Cassell, 2001

— *Rorke's Drift*, Cassell, 2002

Greaves, Adrian and Best, Brian, *The Curling Letters of the Zulu War*, Pen and Sword Books Ltd., 2001

Lowe, John, *Rivalry and Accord 1870–1914*, Hodder & Stoughton, 1990

Mitton, Lavinia, *The Victorian Hospital*, Shire Publications, 1985

Moorehead, Caroline, *Dunant's Dream*, Harper Collins, 1998

Morris, Peter (Ed.), *First Aid to the Battlefront*, Sutton Publishing, 1992

Nightingale, Florence, *Notes on Nursing*, Dover Publications, 1860

Oliver, Beryl, *The British Red Cross in Action*, Faber & Faber, 1966

Ollier, Edmund, *Cassell's History of the Russo-Turkish War*, Cassell, 1878

Parker, Freda, *Victoriana*, Collins, Brown (Blitz edition), 1994

Reader's Digest, *Journeys into the past – Life in the Victorian Age*, 1993

Seaman, L.C.B., *From Vienna to Versailles*, Methuen, 1960

Summers, Anne, *Angels and Citizens – British Women as Military Nurses 1854 – 1914*, Threshold Press, 2000

Taylor, Eric, *Wartime Nurse: One Hundred Years from the Crimea to Korea 1854–1954*, Robert Hale, 2001

Thompson, Carl, *Dawn*, Dowding, 1922

Wantage, Lord, *A Memoir by Lady Wantage*, pub. unk., 1907

Watkin, Brian, *The Prince of Wales General Hospital – A Centenary History*, pub. unk., 1967

Woodham Smith, Cecil, *Florence Nightingale*, Constable, 1950

Newspapers and Periodicals 1878–9

The Times

The Daily Telegraph

The Natal Witness

The Illustrated London News

The Graphic

Modern Journals

Journals 1 – 17 of the Anglo Zulu War Historical Society
Sunday Times Magazine, Perry, George & Mason, Nicholas (Eds.) *Rule Britannia – The Victorian World*

Diaries and scrapbooks

Those of Janet Wells and members of her family

Contemporary Journals and Reports

Operations of the British National Society for the Aid to the Sick and Wounded in War during the Russo-Turkish War 1877–77 published London 1878
British Medical Journal report of the Committee on the Army Medical Services 1878
Stafford House reports 1880

Index of Names